Why Do We STRUGGLE So?

EBED
PUBLICATIONS

In love, serve one another

Carol

Ja 5:14
De 28:1-14

by

Carol Hill Richardson

EBED Publications is a ministry of The McDougal Foundation, Inc., a Maryland nonprofit corporation dedicated to spreading the Gospel of the Lord Jesus Christ to as many people as possible in the shortest time possible.

Published by:

ƐBƐD Publications
P.O. Box 3595
Hagerstown, MD 21742-3595

ISBN 1-884369-44-8

First Printing 1997
Second Printing 1998

Printed in the United States of America
For Worldwide Distribution

DEDICATION

To Jim, my patient and kind husband, of more than thirty-five years, and to our children, Chelly and Craig, who chose their mates, Tim and Jennifer, carefully and well. I love you all, each one of you God's chosen, and dedicate to you this work.

ACKNOWLEDGMENTS

I know the power of the printed word. In 1971, the book, *Prison to Praise*, by Merlin Carothers, pointed my life in the right direction. Thank you, Alice Boseman, for giving me that book. Thanks also to my friends, Ruth Heflin, and her brother, the late Rev. Wallace Heflin (who went to be with the Lord on December 27, 1996), for their advice and for pointing me in the right direction with *Why Do We Struggle So?*

This book is the result of taking dozens of tapes from my daily radio broadcast, transcribing them, and editing them into readable form. Much time and labor have gone into transforming the spoken message into a tangible form. I owe a special debt of gratitude to my friends at EBED Publications for their tireless work and for their encouragement along the way. Thank you all for making Psalm 45:1 come true for me: *"My tongue is the pen of a ready writer."*

Thanks also to Dolores Morgan for your gifts of editing, encouragement and much more; to my secretary, Patricia Cox, for everything you've done to make my work easier; to Vernon and Lib Howell, David and Barbara Summerlin, and Horace and Betty Elliott (you know what you did!); to my traveling partner and friend, Archie Brakers, for constantly uplifting me in intercession; to my pastor, Ronald Estes, of the United Methodist Church of Bath, North Carolina, and Maynard Waters of Harvest Church in Washington, North Carolina, for their on-going support and encouragement; and to Bill Zachman, my first Bible teacher. You're still one of the best.

Finally, a big thank you to all my intercessors. I won't attempt to name all of you, because to leave out one name would hurt both you and me. It is in large part due to you that this book has become a reality.

Lest I forget Proverbs 3:6, I acknowledge with heartfelt gratitude, my very precious Lord Jesus Christ. All the glory is Yours!

CONTENTS

FOREWORD BY JIM RICHARDSON

If you were to meet my wife and to sit down and talk with her, you would soon notice several things about her. It wouldn't take you long to see her love for her Lord and to sense her trust and confidence in Him. This would be evident through the things she told you—what the Lord has done in our family and how He is currently working in her own personal life. Like others, you would come to the conclusion that this is a woman who is strong in the Word, in her faith, and in her relationship with the Lord Jesus, and you would be absolutely right. But it was not always so ...

There was a period in our lives when I would leave for work each morning, not knowing what to expect when I returned home that evening. Carol was tormented by such terrible fears. Her fear, of things known and things unknown alike, grew to the point that it consumed her — physically, spiritually, and emotionally.

She was afraid that she would go sleepwalking

and unwittingly harm our children. She was afraid that some group of tourists visiting our historical town would actually be drug-crazed hippies. She was afraid that some evil person was lurking around the school our children attended, wanting to do them harm. Although all of these fears were irrational, nothing I could say or do offered her any comfort, and she cried herself to sleep every night.

We tried many ways of dealing with this terribly incapacitating fear. Tranquilizers didn't help. Locking all the doors and windows of our home and double-checking them each night didn't help. Getting a good watchdog didn't help. And hiding knives and other dangerous items from would-be intruders didn't help. In fact, nothing seemed to help, and with every effort we made, her fears only grew.

Personally, I found it very difficult to understand why my wife would be plagued by such all-consuming fear. After all, our family was healthy, and we were financially stable. We attended church and were involved with civic clubs and school support groups. Why should life be such a struggle?

Then, one day in 1971 Carol read a book entitled *Prison to Praise* by Merlin Carothers. Like a bolt of lightning, the answer to her problem was exposed. There was only one thing missing in Carol's life: the applied blood of Jesus.

As suddenly as the answer was revealed, Carol laid hold of it, and I saw a wonderful change in her that very evening when I arrived home.

I didn't openly question her about her experience at the time. I just accepted with gratitude the fact that her fears had vanished and that she was now filled with peace, joy and happiness. But it was a remarkable change that had taken place in just a few hours time.

From that day on, Carol began to devour the Scriptures so that she could better understand what had been revealed to her through that book. She wanted to be able to explain it to others. So, the years since then, for Carol, have been an ongoing process of learning, teaching and growing. The Lord was equipping her for ministry.

Carol has now taught Bible study classes in our church since 1979. In 1980 she was certified as a lay speaker. She earned her Bachelor's degree in theology from Christian International College in 1988 and was licensed to preach through the Church of the Redeemer in 1992. She has conducted a daily radio program since March of 1994, has been featured on local television stations, has made mission trips to Russia and the Ukraine, and has also visited Israel.

Carol's example helped to inspire our son to enter the full-time ministry. He received his first church assignment in 1996. So, the legacy of the Lord's work in Carol's life continues.

Why Do We Struggle So? has been written because

of the encouragement of many friends who have shared with us the desire that others might benefit from the teachings in God's Word that so transformed my wife. I trust that it will help bring to many others the same deliverance and joy that I witnessed coming into Carol's life in 1971.

INTRODUCTION

Throughout the world Christians are struggling with difficult situations, problems, and trials (testings), and many are losing the battle. Enough battles lost and a hopelessness sets in. In America there is a very popular saying, "God helps them that help themselves," but what about those who can't help themselves? What about those who are caught up in situations not of their own choosing?

Many people have tried to "help themselves" through dogged determination, others through their reputation, or power, prestige and money, through connections, through the court system, or a host of other ways. But the one sure way that a child of God can help himself is the way that Noah, Abraham, Joseph, Moses, Joshua, Ruth, Gideon, David and a long list of other Bible characters chose. That was to put their trust in a covenant-keeping God and watch as He worked in their behalf. *Why Do We Struggle So?* is a book to remind every Christian that the same God who came to their aid will also come to ours.

What does it mean to be in blood covenant with the God of the Universe? How do we get Him to do battle for us? How do we deal with disappointment and fears and the multitude of "enemies" that come against us?

My prayer is that this book will help you to walk a victorious, joy-filled life by helping you to refocus on a truth easily forgotten in times of conflict. This truth is found in the words of an old hymn, "What a Friend we have in Jesus, *all* our sins and griefs to bear."

Our God *wants* to do battle for us. He *wants* to bear the major part of our burdens. He *wants* us to walk in peace. May this book help you to take hold of long-neglected promises that God has given to benefit all His people.

Carol Hill Richardson
Bath, North Carolina

CHAPTER ONE

FREEDOM FROM STRUGGLE — AT LAST!

I am the way and the truth and the life. No one comes to the Father except through Me.

John 14:6

My discovery of the truth that enabled me to rest in the goodness of God did not come quickly or easily. It took, in fact, twelve very long and trying years.

I had given my life to the Lord as a teenager, kneeling at the altar of a little country church, and had walked with Him for several years after that, learning a few truths from His Word. But I hadn't gone nearly far enough, and I wasn't satisfied in my spiritual experience.

I constantly hungered for something more, something I seemingly could not find in the church I was attending. So, convinced that I knew how to seek after God on my own, I began a journey that would actually take me away from Him and became involved in what is now known as the New Age Movement. I tried Zen Buddhism, reincarnation, the teachings of Edgar Casey, the "deep thoughts" of Indian swamis, yoga, astrology, and other such teachings. You name it, and I tried it.

As strange as it may sound, I thought I was seeking God in all this. I knew that I was genuinely hungry for Him and wanted to know Him better. And if others could not help me to know Him, I would find the depths of His love on my own.

In my search for God, I did what many others have done. Instead of delving into the Bible for myself and letting God speak to me personally through His Word, I laid that Word aside and continued my spiritual quest in other ways. What a terrible mistake!

I had no idea that this journey would take me away from God, and my separation from Him didn't happen all at once. Nevertheless, that was the end result of my willfulness. Without even realizing it, I was turning my back on God, and, little by little, I was abandoning His wisdom and seeking wisdom from men.

I had never realized that there are two sources of wisdom. I thought that wisdom was wisdom and that all wisdom was good. The Apostle James, however, in his letter to the churches, wrote about a wisdom that *"does not come down from heaven."* He said this kind of wisdom is *"earthly, unspiritual, of the devil."* The true wisdom, he declared, *"is first of all pure; then peace-loving, considerate, submissive, full of mercy and good fruit, impartial, and sincere"* (James 3:15-17). Wow! This is the wisdom I needed.

James had begun his letter to the churches with this sound advice:

> *If any of you lacks wisdom, he should ask God,*
> *who gives generously to all without finding fault,*
> *and it will be given to him.*   James 1:5

How simple! When we ask our heavenly Father for wisdom, He gives it to us, willingly and generously, *"without finding fault."* The King James translation says, He *"upbraideth not."* In other words He won't say (as men often do), "Don't you know that already?" Our God is patient, kind, and loving, and He delights in teaching us His truths. But I had yet to learn these facts and was still wandering in some wilderness of my own making.

During the twelve years of my search for truth in the New Age Movement, I never had real peace. In one sense, things seemed to be going well for me. I was married to a good man; we had two wonderful children; we lived comfortably enough; we were in good health. Life was good. So why wasn't I happy?

Something important was missing from my life,

and it took me a long time to realize what that *something* was. It was only after I had reached the point of suicidal fear that I sensed the Lord Jesus Christ reaching out His hand to me. I heard Him say, "Come on home, child. Come on home." And, by God's grace, I came running back into the arms of a Father who had never given up on me and was only waiting for me to recognize my need of Him and to turn back to His loving arms.

God knew my heart. He knew that I had not deliberately walked away from His only way of salvation, but that I was seeking Him in my own way. He also knew that I was stubborn and strong-willed and that I would need some hard experiences to show me that I could not find my way without His help and that I could not seek wisdom outside of His written Word. I thank Him for allowing me to taste of the bitterness of a life void of His Presence, for it caused me to turn back to Him that day.

My homecoming occurred in March of 1971 and, since then, my life has grown more wonderful with each passing day. As the old chorus declares, He is *"sweeter as the days go by."*

I quickly learned that those who walk in God's perfect desire for their lives and who keep themselves tightly yoked to Him, listening to Him and obeying Him, can find absolute peace for every day and for every situation that life may present. We have no reason to struggle when He is on our side.

18

Freedom From Struggle — At Last!

That isn't to say that we have no more battles. We do! But God is our Defender, ready to do battle for us at any moment. As our loving heavenly Father, He takes complete responsibility for our welfare — which includes fighting for us when necessary.

I am not suggesting that God is at our beck and call. By no means! We were created and placed here on this earth for His pleasure, not He for ours. John wrote:

> *Thou art worthy, O Lord, to receive glory and honour and power: for Thou hast created all things, and for Thy pleasure they are and were created.* Revelation 4:11, KJV

"All things" that have been created are for God's pleasure. If you have ever wondered, "Why am I here?" or "What is life all about?" this is the Lord's comforting reply to you. You were created for His pleasure, and you will find your fulfillment as you find union with Him.

When God decided to create mankind, it was with the thought of having fellowship with His creation:

> *We proclaim to you what we have seen and heard, so that you also may have fellowship with us. And our fellowship is with the Father and with His Son, Jesus Christ.* 1 John 1:3

Why Do We Struggle So?

We were first conceived in the heart of God and, therefore, have a definite purpose in His economy. He is our Father and, like every good father, desires that His children spend time with Him, talk with Him, and, more importantly, heed His advice. Learning to listen to God can save us so much heartbreak. It can take all the struggle out of our lives. Unfortunately, most of us find that out the hard way.

The day that I came to realize that the way to God is not through all the means that men have devised, but through His Son Jesus Christ, I was on my way to finding complete rest in the Lord. I am grateful that I found my way back to God and that my personal struggle has ceased.

CHAPTER TWO

GOD — OUR GREAT DEFENDER

*Moses answered the people, "Do not be afraid.
Stand firm and you will see the deliverance the
Lord will bring you today. The Egyptians you see
today you will never see again. The Lord will fight
for you; you need only to be still."*

Exodus 14:13-14

After I returned to the Lord, one of the truths that
He birthed into my spirit is that He is on our side.
He had not been purposefully hiding from me. He
was simply waiting for me to come to Him on His
terms. I thought I had been battling to get to God,
but what I didn't realize was that God was doing
battle for me. He is our Defender and Champion.
Champion is defined as "one who defends, fights for,
or supports a cause or another person." Goliath was
a champion of the Philistines, but David was able
to defeat him because he knew that God was Champion of Israel.

Why Do We Struggle So?

When Moses had led the people of Israel out of their slavery in Egypt, the armies of Pharaoh pursued them, thinking to place them back into bondage. The sight of that powerful force approaching must have been terrifying. And what could they do? They had no chariots, no horses, and no weapons. They were untrained in warfare. How could they defend themselves?

Yet Moses was not afraid and told the children of Israel not to be afraid either. They were, after all, God's people, and God would fight for them. They should just remain still and watch what God was about to do to their enemies.

It happened just as Moses had said. The armies of Pharaoh were destroyed in the Red Sea that day and were no longer a threat to God's people.

The idea of God doing battle for us may seem farfetched to some. After all, many of us were taught to believe the old adage, "God helps them that help themselves." While this saying does contain a certain amount of truth, many people have taken it to the extreme. We may think that a display of independence, "doing it my way," shows strength, but that is a serious mistake. True strength is being able to say to God, who is our Creator, "Father, I will not attempt to do this thing without You. Allow me to keep my neck under Your yoke, so that You can do the major part of the work. Let me always cast my cares on You, because I know You care for me."

When victory comes, therefore, we can always say, "To God be the glory"; for He is our Great Defender and Champion.

Our God is a warrior God who is more than willing to do battle for us. He is the same God who brought Moses and the children of Israel out of Egypt, and the same God who destroyed Pharaoh and his armies in the Red Sea. He has not changed. He is still *"the same"*:

> *Jesus Christ is the same yesterday and today and forever.* Hebrews 13:8

To some, the compassionate Christ of the New Testament cannot be the same as the God of the Old Testament, full of wrath and vengeance. But that image never was a true picture of our God. He has always been loving and compassionate.

Yes, God is demanding. Yes, He holds His people to a high standard. But that is not because He is lacking in compassion, but rather because He wants the very best for each of us. The demands He makes on us were never meant to take the joy out of our lives, but to enhance every life experience.

The God of Moses is fully revealed through the goodness and compassion of the Christ of the New Testament. Jesus Himself said:

> *Anyone who has seen me has seen the Father.* John 14:9

Because we serve the God of Moses, I firmly believe that the promises given to the children of Israel in Old Testament times may be received by those who love our God today. Those blessings were destined for men and women of all ages, through Christ:

> *Christ redeemed us from the curse of the law by becoming a curse for us, for it is written: "Cursed is everyone who is hung on a tree." He redeemed us in order that the blessing given to Abraham might come to the Gentiles through Christ Jesus, so that by faith we might receive the promise of the Spirit.* Galatians 3:13-14

Our covenant with God through Christ contains even better promises than did the Old Covenant:

> *But the ministry Jesus has received is as superior to theirs [that of the Levitical priesthood] as the covenant of which He is mediator is superior to the old one, and it is founded on better promises.* Hebrews 8:6

The same God who comforted the children of Israel as they stood by the Red Sea, contemplating their fate at the hands of Pharaoh, stands with you today. He says to you, "You will not need to fight. Stand still and see what I will do for you." God is your Defender and Champion.

God — Our Great Defender

God is ready to overcome the oppression in your life. He is ready to do battle with the enemy that threatens your welfare. He is more than able to conquer such enemies as frustration, resentment, addiction, envy, depression, anger, sickness — and all the other enemies we face on a regular basis. The God of Moses, who is the God of Carol, and who is your God if you love Him, is ready to give you victory over all these things.

In my own life, fear was the primary enemy. It is something that we all face from time to time, and it can be paralyzing and totally disruptive, robbing us of all our joy and strength. But the Lord is more than able to defeat that enemy. As my Defender, He delivered me from all fear.

Moses declared to the sons of Israel:

The Lord is a warrior; the Lord is His name.
Exodus 15:3

Numbers 21:14 mentions *"the Book of the Wars of the Lord."* Our Great Defender has fought so many battles for His people that an entire book had to be written about His exploits!

Since God has not changed, no battle is too hard for Him today, but sometimes we need to be reminded of that fact. In later years, Moses had to remind the children of Israel of God's fierceness in battle and His ability to deliver His people:

> *Then I said to you, "Do not be terrified; don't be*
> *afraid of them. The Lord your God, who is going*
> *before you, will fight for you, as He did for you in*
> *Egypt."*   Deuteronomy 1:29-30

We might wonder why God's people had to face so many trials of their faith. The truth is that God is always seeking our good, even when the going gets rough. Hear Him, as He speaks to Israel at the end of forty years of wilderness wandering:

> *"Remember how the Lord your God led you all*
> *the way in the desert these many years, to humble*
> *you and to test you in order to know what was in*
> *your heart, whether or not you would keep His*
> *commands."*   Deuteronomy 8:2

When the children of Israel were ready to move into the Promised Land, suddenly the presence of giants living there seemed to prevent them. If they were to take the Promised Land and receive their rightful inheritance from the Lord, they would have to face those giants and overcome them.

Moses had sent twelve spies into the land, and ten of them came back so awed by the enormity of the men they had seen that they warned Moses not to attempt to take the land:

> *We are like grasshoppers in their sight.*
>   Numbers 13:33

God — Our Great Defender

Moses, however, was not deterred by this reaction. He knew God, and he knew that no giant could defy God. "Don't be afraid of them," he said.

Moses was not relying on the strength of the armies of Israel or the valor of her men, but solely on the ability of the nation's Great Defender.

The Lord your God, who is going before you, will fight for you, as He did for you in Egypt, before your very eyes, and in the desert. There you saw how the Lord your God carried you, as a father carries his son, all the way you went until you reached this place. Deuteronomy 1:30-31

The fact that ten of the twelve spies had a negative opinion of the possibility of taking the land had an adverse affect on many of the people, and the Promised Land would remain unconquered for many years to come. Fear is a terrible thing. It robs us of so many blessings that we should rightfully be enjoying.

And so the people wandered in the wilderness, allowing their fear to prevent them from entering into their Promised Land, when, all the while, the Great Defender was among them, ready to do battle with every giant.

Perhaps the reason the children of Israel failed to go forward that day to possess their land is the same reason we are still struggling with life's giants. We sometimes fail to recognize that God is with us. If this is the case in your life, let me assure you that He is on your side — as long as you are on His! All He asks is that we trust Him, even when we don't understand all that is going on in our lives. Trust Him today and call on Him to help you. He will not fail to carry you to safer ground, *"as a man carries his son."* His love for you is as great as His love for Israel. He wants to come to your aid and rescue you from every enemy. Won't you cry out to Him today?

CHAPTER THREE

PARTNERS IN COVENANT
— WITH HIM

This cup is the new covenant in my blood; do this,
whenever you drink it, in remembrance of me.

1 Corinthians 11:25

Why does God fight for us? How can we be so sure that He is our Defender? Why is He on our side? Because we are partners with Him in covenant and, therefore, He cannot do otherwise, as long as we are walking in obedience to His commands. Remember, all His commands are wrapped up in love. Romans 13:10 says:

Love does no harm to its neighbor. Therefore love
is the fulfillment of the law.

Covenant is one of the most prominent themes

found throughout the Scriptures. If we are to understand the Bible, and if we are to properly understand our relationship with God, we must understand what covenant means.

A covenant is "an agreement or contract between two people or two groups of people." What is unique about our covenant with God is that it is signed and sealed in Christ's own blood. It is a blood covenant.

In Bible days, a blood covenant was the most serious type of covenant and, perhaps, the most common. It was more than a simple legal agreement. When two people entered into a blood covenant, everything they were and everything they owned — all their strengths and weaknesses, all their abilities and liabilities — then belonged to their partner in covenant. By the same token, all that the partner had now belonged to them.

The Hebrew word used in the Bible for covenant is *berith* and means "to cut until blood flows." The very act of entering into a covenant among the Hebrews implied the shedding of blood and was a serious agreement.

Blood covenants were so sacred that they not only involved the parties making them, but the heirs of those parties, as well. The covenant was passed down through succeeding generations. This is the reason the Bible speaks of our decisions affecting our heirs *"unto the third and fourth generation"* (Exodus 20:5).

Blood covenants were extremely important to ancient cultures, and all primitive religions incorporated some form of the tradition. The concept was central, for instance, to the traditions of the tribes of Africa, and such covenants were so highly regarded that they were rarely, if ever, disregarded or broken.

One aspect of the blood covenant that made it so important to such cultures was that of *protection*. Life was fragile and lawlessness abounded, so that men needed assurances of safety.

The famous British explorer of Africa, Sir Henry Morton Stanley, better known simply as "Mr. Stanley," entered into blood covenants with more than fifty tribes during his travels on the continent. When he found himself in unfamiliar or hostile territory, among people who did not know him, all he needed to do was to roll up his sleeve, and there, plainly written on his arm, was the record of his covenants with the tribes—inscribed in the scars of bloodletting. These covenants afforded him the protection he needed.

Any of the tribes who had covenant with him would fight for him, if need be. Therefore, the marks of covenant upon his body served as his passport to the unexplored regions of Africa and gave him the freedom he needed to move about the continent. When we enter into covenant with God, we need fear no one.

The physical security or protection that men derived from the blood covenant had an added blessing. It also offered a measure of *financial security.*

Those who entered into blood covenant did not always trust each other implicitly, but uniting with someone else made them stronger against their immediate rivals. Because of this, former enemies often joined forces and fought side by side because a larger enemy had materialized and threatened both parties.

When we enter into covenant with the God of the Universe, what greater security could we seek?

A third reason that the ancients entered into blood covenant was that it afforded them a sense of companionship. Often, those who forged such vows genuinely loved one another and would fight and die for each other. A wonderful biblical example can be found in the account of the friendship shared by David and Jonathan:

> *And it was so, when he had finished speaking to Saul, that the soul of Jonathan was knit to the soul of David, and Jonathan loved him as his own soul. Saul took him that day, and would not let him go home to his father's house anymore. Then Jonathan and David made a covenant, because he loved him as his own soul. And Jonathan took off the robe that was on him and gave it to David, with his armor, even to his sword and his bow and his belt.* 1 Samuel 18:1-4

Partners In Covenant — With Him

The majority of the covenants described in the Old Testament were made precisely because of similar bonds of love, because the covenants were initiated by God and were covenants with and among His people. To those involved in the covenant, the other benefits were just side issues.

In ancient times there were several steps involved in making such a serious covenant. First, the two people or two groups of people would come together, and there would be an exchange of coats and weaponry. The exchange of clothing implied, "This is who I am. All that I am, I give to you." The exchange of weapons implied, "This is my strength, and I'm giving it to you. If your enemies come out against you, it will be as if they had come against me personally. I will come to your aid." There would also be an exchange of names, and a part of each participant's name would be given to the other.

There would be bloodletting, usually at the wrist or the palm of the hand, but sometimes above the elbow. If it was done at the wrist, a cut would be made on the wrist of each man, and then the two would join their wrists together and allow their blood to mingle. If the cut was made on the palm of the hands, then the two would shake hands to allow their blood to mix. If the cut was made above the elbow, the parties would let the blood drip into a glass of wine. Then the wine became part of the covenant meal.

Animals were also sacrificed, their bodies laid so that their blood flowed together. The two parties entering into covenant walked in and around and among these pieces of flesh in a figure eight. As they did so, they walked through the blood, declaring blessings on those who kept the covenant, and curses on those who broke it. (Read Deuteronomy 28:1-14 to get an idea of some of the covenantal promises God made to the Israelites. These are our promises too if we believe Galatians 3 and appropriate them by faith in Jesus Christ. The curses for breaking covenant are found in verses 15-68.)

After this invocation of blessings and curses, the two parties set up a memorial. It might have been nothing more than a particular stone, but it would serve to remind all the concerned parties of their blood covenant.

Sometimes they gave each other a few sheep to start a flock or a few trees to start a forest, both of which would serve to remind each party of the blood covenant commitment.

After setting up the memorial, the two parties would sit down together to a simple meal, usually bread and wine. As they partook of the food and drink, each would take turns serving the other. One would say, "This is my body. This is my blood. Eat it. Drink it." Then the second person would do the same. As they shared the simple meal, they were symbolically partaking of each other.

Partners In Covenant — With Him

This should sound very familiar to most of us, since we often share a blood covenant meal with our fellow believers in Christ. Paul described it in detail in his first letter to the Corinthians:

The Lord Jesus, on the night he was betrayed, took bread, and when he had given thanks, he broke it and said, "This is my body, which is for you; do this in remembrance of me."

In the same way, after supper he took the cup, saying, "This cup is the new covenant in my blood; do this, whenever you drink it, in remembrance of me." For whenever you eat this bread and drink this cup, you proclaim the Lord's death until he comes.

Therefore, whoever eats the bread or drinks the cup of the Lord in an unworthy manner will be guilty of sinning against the body and blood of the Lord. A man ought to examine himself before he eats of the bread and drinks of the cup. For anyone who eats and drinks without recognizing the body of the Lord eats and drinks judgment on himself. That is why many among you are weak and sick, and a number of you have fallen asleep.

1 Corinthians 11:23-30

When we receive Jesus Christ as our Savior, we enter into the covenant that He made on our behalf with the heavenly Father. He became the spotless

Lamb of God and was sacrificed on our behalf, and it was His blood that sets this New Covenant in order.

In Christ, we have also done an exchange of coats and garments. We have taken on the Person of Jesus.

> *For all of you who were baptized into Christ have clothed yourselves with Christ.*   Galatians 3:27

We don't merely believe on Him; He has taken up residence in our lives. Paul described it this way:

> *I have been crucified with Christ and I no longer live, but Christ lives in me. The life I live in the body, I live by faith in the Son of God, who loved me and gave Himself for me.*   Galatians 2:20

We have exchanged our garments of unrighteousness and, in their place, put on God's glory, His robe of righteousness.

In the passage from First Corinthians, Paul wrote that because some believers didn't understand what they were doing, when they accepted the bread and wine of the Lord's blood covenant meal, some had become ill, and others had even died. We might wonder what the Lord's table had to do with physical healing and even death.

When the children of Israel shared their first Passover meal in Egypt, their people had been in bondage there for more than four hundred years. God had sent Moses, however, and was ready to bring the Israelites out of Egypt and to lead them into the Promised Land. To convince Pharaoh to let His people go, God had to send a series of plagues upon Egypt, plagues that greatly troubled the citizens of Egypt while they left the enslaved Hebrews untouched.

In the final plague, God sent the death angel to smite the firstborn son of every Egyptian family. In order to insure that the households of all those who trusted in God remained untouched by the passing of the death angel, God gave instructions on how to be protected.

Each family was to prepare a sacrificial lamb. When the lamb had been slain, they would dip some hyssop in the blood of the lamb and then strike it on the lintel and door posts of their houses. God promised that when He saw the blood he would *"pass over"* that home:

> *For the Lord will pass through to smite the Egyptians; and when He seeth the blood upon the lintel, and on the two side posts, the Lord will pass over the door, and will not suffer the destroyer to come in unto your houses to smite you.*
>
> Exodus 12:23, KJV

The term *pass over* in this passage meant much

more than simply that the Lord would *"pass over"* the house. It meant, "The Lord will hover; He will halt; He will hesitate." God was saying that He would come and stand between Israel and all her enemies, not just the death angel. He would be a covering, a protection, to His people, standing between them and anyone who sought to harm them. The blood of our Passover Lamb, Jesus Christ, offers us the same protection. It is His blood — not our money, our power, our prestige, our denomination, our looks, our race, or anything else — that stands between us and our enemies.

Four hundred years of slavery brought with it untold suffering. The people were, no doubt, afflicted with many diseases. As slaves, they were rarely permitted to bathe, their diet was poor, and they worked under harsh taskmasters who had no mercy on them and no concern for their physical welfare.

Later, God was to say to them:

> *The Lord will keep you free from every disease. He will not inflict on you the horrible diseases you knew in Egypt.* Deuteronomy 7:15

The miracle had already begun when Moses led the people forth:

> *He brought them forth also with silver and gold:*

and there was not one feeble person among their tribes.   Psalm 105:37, KJV

How is this possible? This was a very large group of people. They had been badly treated, poorly fed, and overworked for long years. Yet there was not a single sickly person among them. What a miracle!

I am convinced that the miracle came as they partook of the Passover Lamb, because there is healing in the Lamb, as the prophets foretold:

By his wounds we are healed.   Isaiah 53:5

When you receive the Lord's Supper, when you partake of that bread and that wine, remember this: You are partaking of the Lamb and of His shed blood, and, for you and me, there is healing in the Lamb.

This very passage is quoted by Peter as part of the New Testament, so we know that this promise of healing was not just for Old Testament times. We can have these benefits of covenant today, and I have seen this truth at work — many times.

When I first came to the Lord, at the altar of that little country church in Arkansas, that Wednesday night in my fifteenth year, there was such a drastic change in my life that my mother went to the same church that Friday night and got saved herself. The two of us were baptized together the following Sunday.

My mom had suffered terrible migraines for as long as I could remember, but from the moment she received Jesus as her Lord and Savior, from the moment she partook of the Lamb, she never had another migraine, to my remembrance.

Not everyone experiences such a dramatic healing of every sickness. Some are healed progressively. As we mature, I find that the Lord requires more perseverance on our part and insists that we seek Him as part of the healing process. But we are healed, nevertheless.

We must continue to affirm, "Jesus bore my suffering, my pain, my sorrows, and my sickness in His own body on that tree. I know what God has promised and, because I love Him and trust Him and because He is my covenant God, I believe that He will continue to heal me in my areas of need."

His sacrifice on Calvary was for much more than our physical ailments. The prophet wrote:

> *Surely He hath borne our griefs, and carried our sorrows: yet we did esteem Him stricken, smitten of God, and afflicted. But He was wounded for our transgressions, He was bruised for our iniquities: the chastisement of our peace was upon Him; and with His stripes we are healed.*
>
> Isaiah 53:4-5, KJV

Jesus bore our *sorrows*. The Hebrew word used

here means "shame, guilt, and failure." Thank God He bore it all. Don't hold on to any embarrassment, feeling of rejection, or disappointment. Give it all to our Savior. He has already borne the pain caused by it and wants you to receive your healing now.

CHAPTER FOUR

FACING OUR SIN
— BUT NOT ALONE

*If we confess our sins, He is faithful and just and
will forgive us our sins and purify us from all
unrighteousness.*   1 John 1:9

A common enemy we all face is our own tendency
to sin. And, as if the sin itself were not enough, the
enemy seeks to use our weakness to his advantage,
to make us turn away from God in shame. The devil
is a liar and the father of lies. If you have been feeling that God surely cannot forgive you again for that
same sin you have committed over and over, if you
have been thinking that He cannot use you for any
good purpose because of your imperfections, if you
think that you have moved beyond the ability of God
to save, you can be sure that the enemy has been
whispering in your ear. If you are a Christian, then

the Christ who triumphed over sin dwells in you, and you are victorious in Him! Jesus was victorious over sin in His life, in His death, and in His resurrection; and He can triumph over sin in us, as well.

What should we do when we discover sin in our lives? The Scriptures are clear: We should confess it, repent of it, ask the Lord's forgiveness for it, and ask Him to help us never to do it again. *"He is faithful and just,"* and He *"will forgive us our sins"* and He will *"purify us from all unrighteousness."* These are powerful promises that we must not take lightly.

God knows the sincerity of your heart. When He hears your penitent prayer, He always answers positively. If you walk humbly before Him, even your own failure cannot prevent the blessing of God from coming upon you. You are victorious through Christ.

Since we have entered into blood covenant with God, through Jesus Christ, our warrior God can and will fight for us. Because of our covenant relationship with Him, *our* enemies are *His* enemies. One of my favorite scriptures is Deuteronomy 28:7:

> *The Lord will grant that the enemies who rise up against you will be defeated before you. They will come at you from one direction and flee from you in seven.*

Put God in remembrance of His covenantal promises. It is vital that we do so because it shows that we are trusting in Him. Regardless of what you may be facing in your life, God is on your side — even when you are not perfect.

The testimony of Old Testament kings who faced serious enemies are examples in this regard. Hezekiah was one of Judah's godly kings. When enemies threatened his kingdom, he presented himself before the people and challenged them with these words:

> *Be strong and courageous. Do not be afraid or discouraged because of the king of Assyria and the vast army with him, for there is a greater power with us than with him. With him is only the arm of flesh, but with us is the Lord our God to help us and to fight our battles.* 2 Chronicles 32:7-8

We may not have a physical enemy with armies marching toward us, but we certainly have emotional enemies that are equally as dangerous and threatening, and we can cling to this promise, as well. He will *"help us."* He will *"fight our battles."*

The New Testament counterpart to this promise was given through John to the Church:

> *Greater is He that is in you, than he that is in the world.*   1 John 4:4, KJV

Regardless of what enemy is coming against you,

know one thing: the power of your enemy cannot compare with that of the Lord God Almighty who dwells within you, if you have received Jesus Christ. Resist the temptation to panic, and simply ask God to come to your aid, to rise up against your enemies. He will help you. He is not just up in Heaven somewhere. He lives in you.

God is omnipotent, omniscient, and omnipresent — all-powerful, all-knowing, and in all places. He is with you always, wherever you may be. Call out to Him when you find yourself in trouble. Say to Him, "Oh God, I can't do this myself. I need Your help!" He will not despise your weakness, but will show you His strength in the midst of your weakness. And He will put weapons in your hands that will enable you to overcome every enemy.

Let us look at some of the secret weapons God has given us by looking at another king, King Jehoshaphat of Judah. At one point, three great enemies — the Moabites, the Ammonites, and the Meunites — joined in a war against this godly man. When Jehoshaphat heard of it, he looked to God, calling the people together to seek the Lord in a solemn assembly. When the people came together out of all the cities of Judah, the king personally led them in fasting and prayer to the Almighty. This is a wonderful example for each of us to follow.

If you have never fasted or have done it infrequently, you are robbing yourself of one of the most powerful spiritual weapons that God has given to the Church. Oh, you are not alone. Fasting has practically become a lost art among modern Christians. Yet it has many benefits, both physical and spiritual. God has required that fasting be part of our seeking Him.

Jesus did not say to His disciples, "If you fast ... ," He said, *"When you fast ..."* (Matthew 6:17). He expected His people to fast, just as surely as He expected them to pray or to give.

Fasting enables us to put our bodies into subjection so that our spirits can touch the hem of the Master's garment. It clears the way for us to be able to hear the voice of God more effectively. It shows our seriousness before Him.

Fasting is not a form of spiritual arm-twisting, and it's not an attempt to force God to do what we want. It is positioning ourselves to hear God and to cooperate with Him, to know and fulfill His perfect will in our lives.

The children of Israel fasted corporately — that is, they all fasted together, at the same time. It is important that we fast with other believers from time to time, as well as fasting on our own as individuals. We will investigate the power of fasting more fully in a later chapter.

The second response of Jehoshaphat and his people was to publicly call out to the Lord in prayer. This is an important step. Our Lord is more precious to us than any lost treasure, and we must give time and energy to seeking His face. He has promised that He will answer your call:

Ask and it will be given to you; seek and you will find; knock and the door will be opened to you.
                                                          Matthew 7:7

God is always present, whether we feel His presence or not. Sometimes He may remove the consciousness of His presence for a time, to see what our response will be. When this happens, we must not waver or doubt. He is present. He hears our cry, and He will answer us. He is only testing our sincerity. Continuing to seek Him shows our determination to have His best in our lives.

As he prayed, Jehoshaphat acknowledged Judah's need of the Lord:

We do not know what to do, but our eyes are upon you.   2 Chronicles 20:12

This was a wonderful position to take, and it assured success for the king. If there is any one thing that will guarantee our success in life, it is keeping our eyes focused on the Lord. Some of us have our minds so focused on the events of the day and are so moved by them that we can no longer stay focused on what God is saying. We are focusing on the problem instead of the solution, and that is deadly. Let us keep our eyes on Jesus, for He is bigger than any problem we might face.

When you are not sure of exactly how you should pray in a given situation, don't worry about it. Just focus your eyes on the Lord. Confess to Him that you don't know what to say, or what to ask for, or how to give Him your burdens —because you don't understand them yourself. He will come to your aid.

Spending time worshiping the Lord is far more important than presenting Him with your wish list. Focus on Him and on His promises, and as you focus on Him, be sensitive to hear what He might speak to you. You will be surprised. He has much to say to each of us — if we are willing to listen.

We all experience moments in which we literally don't know what to do, but if we recognize that God does know what to do, we come one step closer to victory.

Keep praising the Lord in every situation.

There was another secret which the people of Judah now employed:

All the men of Judah, with their wives and children and little ones, stood there before the Lord.
2 Chronicles 20:13

What an amazing statement! These were busy people. They had a lot to do. Their lives were in imminent danger. Yet they *"all"* just *"stood there before the Lord."* To me, this is one of the greatest secrets of overcoming every enemy in our lives (and one that we find hardest to employ these days) — waiting on the Lord.

Jehoshaphat had fasted and prayed. He had praised God. Now, there was nothing left for him to do but wait. Waiting seems to be so hard for us in these closing days of the twentieth century. We are all so busy, so programmed, so scheduled. We don't have time to wait. Yet, God requires that we wait before Him and allow Him to work in His own way and in His own time:

> But they that wait upon the Lord shall renew their strength; they shall mount up with wings as eagles; they shall run, and not be weary; and they shall walk, and not faint.　　Isaiah 40:31, KJV

The Hebrew phrase translated *they that wait* means "those who are braided together with God; those who have allowed Him to be the strong strand." If we hope to succeed in life, we must be bound up, or braided together with God's strong strand. We give Him our weakness and, in return, He gives us His strength. We give Him our fears and, in return, He gives us His courage. We give Him our lack and, in return, He gives us His bounty. Wow! This is worth the wait. Allow yourself to be braided together with God. Lean on Him, and He will be your strength.

Facing Our Sin —But Not Alone

The public prayer of King Jehoshaphat had not been a motivational tool to stir the people to action or to get them psyched up for battle. He was truly seeking God's help, and now he expected God to come to his rescue and was willing to give God time to work. The king could wait, and he would not be disappointed, for waiting on God in this way and expecting His answer is just as important a part of prayer as the asking itself. Jehoshaphat had reminded God that because they were descendants of Abraham the land belonged to Judah, not to the enemy armies who were advancing toward them. He could wholly lean upon a covenant-keeping God.

There they all stood, waiting to hear what God would say, waiting to see what God would do. And all the while the armies of the enemy were coming ever closer.

As the king and his people waited, God responded to them. Suddenly a prophet stood up in the midst of the people. His name was Jahaziel, and he spoke the word of the Lord for that moment. The first word out of his mouth was so important: *"Listen!"* (1 Chronicles 20:15).

We are sometimes so slow to hear what God is trying to tell us. Because we are so busy listening to everyone else and everything else, we barely have time or patience to hear God. *Listen*! If we would listen to what God is trying to say to us, we would have fewer problems.

When the disciples were on the Mount of Transfiguration with Jesus, they were so excited by what they saw that they wanted to do something. "Oh, let's build three tabernacles," Peter said. It was then that they heard a voice from Heaven, saying:

> *This is my Son ... . Listen to him!*
>
> Matthew 17:5

We take our list of petitions before God, and we read it off to Him, as if He doesn't already know our needs. I wonder sometimes why He even listens to us, but He does.

Yet, when it comes time to reverse the process, when it is time for us to listen to God, many of us fail. This is tragic because what He wants to say to us is so much more important than anything we might say to Him. *Listen!*

And what was it that God wanted to say to His people?

> *Do not be afraid or discouraged because of this vast army. For the battle is not yours, but God's. Tomorrow march down against them. ... Take up your positions; stand firm and see the deliverance the Lord will give you. ... Go out to face them tomorrow, and the Lord will be with you.*
>
> 2 Chronicles 20:15-17

Facing Our Sin —But Not Alone

There can be no mistake. God fights for His people!

What comes next in the biblical narrative is so important to our own ultimate victory:

> *Jehoshaphat bowed with his face to the ground, and all the people of Judah and Jerusalem fell down in worship before the Lord. Then some Levites from the Kohathites and the Korahites stood up and praised the Lord, the God of Israel, with very loud voice.* 2 Chronicles 20:18-19

Humility and praise go together. When we recognize that we are nothing and that God is everything, we are one giant step closer to victory.

This outburst of spontaneous humility and praise from the king and all the people was not just an emotional response to the prophecy that had come forth. The people were genuinely worshiping Him who would bring them deliverance. They were praising Him in whom they had placed their trust. Their lives were in God's hands, and they were happy about that fact. Who's better to trust?

Prayer and fasting, waiting upon the Lord, and hearing His response, are all in vain — if we never learn the importance of obedience. Early the next morning the men of Judah set out for the Desert of Tekoa in obedience to what the Lord had said through His prophet. Jehoshaphat had some parting words for them:

> *As they set out, Jehoshaphat stood and said, "Listen to me, Judah and people of Jerusalem! Have faith in the Lord your God and you will be upheld; have faith in His prophets and you will be successful."*   2 Chronicles 20:20

Faith and obedience go together. If we believe God, we must obey. And why would we not obey? God knows exactly what He is doing, and we cannot lose by following through on His commands.

Often, obeying God requires that we employ some rather unorthodox techniques. At this point, King Jehoshaphat employed a very unusual battle strategy. Instead of sending the infantry first, or the bowmen, or the warriors with spears, he sent a group of worshipers as the advance assault upon the enemy:

> *After consulting the people, Jehoshaphat appointed men to sing to the Lord and to praise Him for the splendor of His holiness as they went out at the head of the army saying: "Give thanks to the Lord, for His love endures forever."*
>
>   2 Chronicles 20:21

The next verse shows us what happened when

these special spiritual soldiers were sent before the armed warriors and began to praise the Lord:

> *As they began to sing and praise, the Lord set ambushes against the men of Ammon and Moab and Mount Seir who were invading Judah, and they were defeated.*   Verse 22

God had a plan for the salvation of His people, and He knew how to carry out that plan successfully. As God's people were obedient to fast, to pray, to hear and obey His word given through His prophet, and to praise the Lord in anticipation of victory, He confused the enemy and caused them to turn on each other. The Ammonites and Moabites began to kill the men of Mount Seir, and when they had finished, they turned on one another. By the time the men of Judah arrived on the scene, all they could see were dead bodies strewn about. Not one enemy soldier remained to fight. *"No one had escaped"* (verse 24). What a wonderful God we serve!

Never fear a battle, for when it is over, you will be able to reap the spoils. Every enemy soldier was dead, so the only thing left for Jehoshaphat and his men to do was to go about gathering up the spoils of battle. That proved to be no easy task. What they found was so abundant that it took them three days to collect it all.

My friend, there are spoils awaiting you and me.

Satan has robbed us for too long. He has stolen our children; he has stolen our marriages; he has stolen our money; and he has stolen our joy. It is now time for restoration. It is time for Satan to repay all that he has stolen. It is time to gather up the spoils of battle.

God is ready, not only to face our enemies and to cause them to back down, but He is also ready to restore to us all that the enemy has stolen through the years. Praise God! It is not that He will cause a divorced husband or wife to come back, though that, too, can happen. It is not that a loved one who has died will come back. But God will see that your rewards of trusting in Him are even greater than you had before. Remember:

> *The Lord blessed the latter part of Job's life more than the first.* Job 42:12

What must the children of Israel have been thinking during those three days it took them just to carry off the plunder of battle? What had begun as a serious threat to their very existence had ended in a blessing for a prosperous future. That's what our God wants to do for every one of His children.

God is on our side! He will fight for us! He doesn't want to see us defeated. He wants us to seek Him, acknowledge His word to us, be a people of praise, wait, and obey ... and then watch as He defeats our every enemy and leaves for us the spoils of battle.

If we can remember these secret weapons and employ them, we can see the ravages of sin repaired and restored in our lives. But whatever happens, if we remain imperfect until He comes, He still loves us and is with us, our Great Defender.

Why not let Him give us the battle plan and then carry it out in the power of His might? The end result will always be victory.

CHAPTER FIVE

ASSURED OF VICTORY
— EVERY TIME

*Now these things [that happened to the Israelites]
occurred as examples to keep us from setting our
hearts on evil things as they did.*

1 Corinthians 10:6

As a believer, I know that when I am experiencing a difficult season, many other Christians are going through the same thing. We are the Body of Christ, and God speaks to us and deals with us on a corporate level, as well as on a personal level. When He is doing specific things in my life, I know that He is also doing the same work in the lives of others and that others would benefit from knowing what God has done for me.

Since we have the assurance that all things work to our benefit, we know that everything God is permitting to happen in our lives is perfecting us, making us more like Jesus.

The devil wants us to get our eyes upon him and concentrate on the agent of change rather than the actual change that is taking place. He wants us to concentrate on our present troubles and take our eyes off the fact that God is in control of our lives and that, in every situation, He reigns supreme.

The best thing we can do when we are experiencing some trial in life, therefore, is to look up to God and say, "Lord, I trust You, and I focus my eyes upon You. I don't understand why I am experiencing this difficulty, but You do. I don't know the answer to my present problems, but You do. I don't know how to win this battle, but I know that You do. I will never stop trusting You."

Although we trust the Lord, we should not expect or attempt to face our battles alone. As members of the Body of Christ, we need each other. Satan is a wolf in sheep's clothing, and wolves always go after the weaker lambs, after those who are lagging behind, or are otherwise separated from the rest of the flock. Attempting to walk this way alone makes us vulnerable to attack, so maintain good fellowship with your brothers and sisters in Christ.

The Exodus period was a crucial one in the history of Israel, as the sons of Israel had been in bondage in Egypt for far too long — Egypt being a type of the world. Most of us also know what it is to be in bondage to this world. We have been bound by its traditions, by its expectations, and by its ideas. We willingly embraced the world, until God said to us, "Come out. I want you in My Kingdom."

Now, although we still live here on the earth, we no longer have the world's system within us. We are under the leadership and authority of Jesus, and we benefit from it in every way.

When we become part of Christ's Kingdom and allow Him to be King of our lives, we come to know His righteousness and His peace. As we are filled with His Spirit, we experience His joy. We bring great joy to His heart, as well. He has always loved us and desired the best for us; therefore He rejoices to see us blessed in His Kingdom.

Israel in the Old Testament was a type, or pattern, of the Church, a blueprint of what we are to be, an example given for us. Just as we are to emulate her good points, we are to learn from her mistakes.

In the Bible we have a long and detailed history of the struggles of the nation of Israel, replete with successes and failures. These set for us examples that help us not to fall into the same errors committed by her sons — as we traverse a way through the wilderness on our way to our own Promised Land.

When the children of Israel left Egypt, they experienced a short period of unusual peace and prosperity. They were loaded down with benefits heaped on them by their fearful Egyptian neighbors, and they went joyously on their way toward their own land and a bright future. Little did they know that the Red Sea stood in their way, that the Egyptian army would pursue them, that they would have to cross through the territory of many unscrupulous and unfriendly tribes, and that they would be tried in many other ways, as well, before they could reach their desired goal. For the time being, they were innocent babes in their new experience with God.

In the same way, God often leads new Christians very gently, until they have gained strength. New babes in Christ are not immediately sent into battle, and often God does special miracles for the newest of believers, to encourage them.

If I need someone to pray for me, and I want an answer right away, I sometimes go to a new Christian, for it seems as though God answers their prayers quickly. They are like newborn babes in the flesh who cry, wanting to be fed, and, because of their innocence and utter helplessness, they get the attention they need.

After we have been walking with the Lord for a time, however, He allows us to have the experience of persevering in prayer. We no longer require an immediate response. We know that God is with us and loves us and will meet our need — in His own time. We, therefore, become less demanding of God, and more trusting of His goodness.

As Israel marched out of Egypt, she experienced

some of the most wonderful miracles of the Bible. God sent His presence before the people in a physical and visible manifestation. By day, it took the form of a pillar of cloud, and, by night, it became a pillar of fire. The pillar afforded them not only guidance, but protection. And, at night, the pillar of fire was their light.

Thank God, He has not changed in this regard. By day and by night, He leads us by His Spirit. When everything seems light and good around us, He is there, and when the dark times come, with their problems and worries, His presence is just as real — or, perhaps, more so. In the darkest moments of our lives, God will always give us enough light to take one step at a time.

When things seem to be going well, we have no problem realizing that God is guiding us. But we must learn that when everything seems to be going wrong, He is still guiding us. We have no reason to fear when night comes. We have no reason for panic when we approach life's Red Seas. We are safe under His guidance and we need only follow Him, one step at a time.

After he had allowed the Israelites to go, Pharaoh had second thoughts. The loss of such a valuable work force was unacceptable. He simply must bring them back. Therefore, he called for his army, the finest army in the world at that time.

Egypt was very discriminating in selecting men

for her armed forces, accepting only the most valiant as potential soldiers. Then she took those uniquely qualified men and trained them well. The Egyptian soldiers were renowned for their discipline.

The day Pharaoh sent them out to bring back his slaves, they had with them six hundred of their best chariots among their advance troops. Surely they could not fail.

When they had finally overtaken the fleeing Hebrew slaves, they were approaching the Red Sea. When the children of Israel looked back and saw the dust of the approaching armies, they must have been terrified. We think we have problems, but think about hundreds of chariots and thousands of enemy soldiers chasing you. It is difficult to imagine how frightened they must have been. Yet, sometimes we feel just as threatened.

Now, what we do in situations such as these means all the difference between victory and defeat. If we concentrate too much on the problem, it gets heavy, and we can become discouraged. God is saying to us, "Don't look at the problem. Look at Me. Turn away from the problem, and turn to Me." This, in effect, is exactly what Moses said to the people that day:

Do not be afraid. Stand firm and you will see the

Assured of Victory — Every Time

deliverance the Lord will bring you today. ... The
Lord will fight for you; you need only be still.
                                      Exodus 14:13-14

That may sound a bit too simple for some. We feel as if we need to *do* something — and quick. We get so anxious, so caught up in our fears. Our temples begin to throb, our hearts start racing, and we can't seem to think straight, as a feeling of utter helplessness overtakes us.

But helplessness is not a bad feeling when God is on your side. I am willing any day of the week to stand aside and let Him do the work for me. And He is saying to every one of us, "Let Me fight your battle for you. Turn your face toward Me. Fix your gaze upon Me and watch Me as I defeat all your enemies. Don't be afraid. Just trust Me." Why is it that we have such difficulty trusting God? He has never changed, and just as He fought for Israel at the Red Sea, He wants to fight our battles for us today.

What God told the children of Israel to do that day was very simple. One man, Moses, had to stretch out his arms over the sea. It was a simple act of faith, but as Moses obeyed, deliverance came.

All that night, the Lord sent a wind to blow over the sea, dividing the waters, to create a path for the Israelites to cross. And all the fleeing men and women and boys and girls could do was to watch and wait. What a night that must have been!

In one sense, the Hebrews were left with little choice. They could either trust God and walk in faith, or they could die at the hand of the enemy or be carried back into slavery in Egypt. Not much of a choice! They had to go forward. They had to trust God. They were desperate. They had to believe.

Whether you get that desperate or not, God is able to blow away every obstacle in your life with the wind of His Spirit and to make a clear path ahead for you to follow:

> *The waters were divided, and the Israelites went through the sea on dry ground, with a wall of water on their right and on their left. The Egyptians pursued them.* Exodus 14:21-23

What the Israelites didn't know was that the Egyptians were just as frightened as they were — and for good reason. They had witnessed the plagues and knew that God had brought His people forth *"with a mighty hand and an outstretched arm."* Some of them said:

> *Let's get away from the Israelites! The Lord is fighting for them against Egypt.* Exodus 14:25

And they were right. They were all about to die, for when Moses was commanded to stretch out his arm a second time over the sea, and he obeyed, the waters surged back into place, drowning every remnant of the mighty Egyptian army. And if God could do that for His people then, He can fight for you, defeat your every enemy, lift your burdens, cares, and worries and give you peace and joy and hope in their place.

You may think that everything that *can* go wrong *is* going wrong in your life, but if you turn your face toward God, He will push back the clouds and show you the silver lining. Tell Him, "Lord, I have no more strength, and I don't even know how to begin fighting this battle. I turn to You, and because I trust You, I'm going to praise You now for victory."

You may not tremble, as some do in His presence. You may not weep, as others do. That's okay. You may not even feel as if you have much faith. We all experience our moments of weakness in this regard, and God knows that. But He is ready to help you.

You may have some doubts. We all do. Having a doubt is not the same as the sin of "unbelief." Unbelief means you choose not to believe in God. When hard times come and we are robbed of our strength and ability to cope with life's situations, we all pass through moments of doubt. But our faith is maturing, and God accepts us wherever we happen to be at the moment in our journey of faith.

What are you waiting for? Receive His love. Receive His hope. Receive the abundant life He offers you now.

It was not enough for the Lord to bring His people out of Egypt; He wanted to bring them into the land of promise, Canaan. As they proceeded toward that goal, He led them day by day, providing for them whatever they needed — from food and water, to health, to sandals that miraculously never wore out. Eventually the people came to the Wilderness of Paran.

After they had arrived at Paran, the Lord instructed Moses to send spies into the land of Canaan to bring back a report of what they found there. Moses chose a leader from each tribe and sent them, as the Lord had instructed.

When the twelve spies were satisfied that they had seen enough of the land, they returned and issued their report. It had both encouraging and discouraging elements to it:

> *We went into the land to which you sent us, and it does flow with milk and honey! ... But the people who live there are powerful. ... We seemed like grasshoppers in our own eyes, and we looked the same to them.* Numbers 13:27-28 and 33

As we have already seen, ten of the spies were of the opinion that it was impossible to enter the Promised Land. But two of the men, Caleb and Joshua, were sure that God's people could possess all that

He had promised them. After all, He was with them and had led them this far.

Moses himself was not swayed by the bad report. Many years later, when he reminded a new generation of the sending of the spies and their report, he failed to even mention the advice of the ten pessimists and, instead, concentrated on the advice of the two who had returned with a positive attitude ... just as if the others had never spoken (see Deuteronomy 1:22-25).

Historically, the ten men with a negative report existed and were five times more numerous than those with the positive report. Yet Moses was led to relate the words of the two and to forget the words of the ten. We must do the same today. Decide to believe the Word of God even when circumstances don't agree.

The ten men felt like grasshoppers and thought their enemies must have seen them as grasshoppers, too. And so, instead of being the godly leaders that they were meant to be, they became men *"of little faith,"* grasshopper-sized faith.

Like Moses, we must disregard the pessimists of this world and follow closely the Joshuas and Calebs among us. If God says we can take the country, then we can take the country — no matter what others say. "No retreat!" must be our constant battle cry. "Forward into battle! We are on the winning side!" This was Moses' attitude as he continued his narrative to the new generation:

Why Do We Struggle So?

Then I said to you, "Do not be terrified; do not be afraid of them. The Lord your God, who is going before you, will fight for you, as He did for you in Egypt, before your very eyes, and in the desert. There you saw how the Lord your God carried you, as a father carries his son, all the way you went until you reached this place." In spite of this, you did not trust in the Lord your God ... .

Deuteronomy 1:29-32

Forty years had gone by as the children of Israel continued to wander in the wilderness, and a new generation needed to know how graciously God had dealt with His people and why they had not moved on to the Promised Land. They had been slow to trust the very God who had delivered them.

Now, they were ready, at last, to cross over the Jordan River and into Canaan, but Moses was saying his final farewells; for he would not be accompanying them. God had set a very high standard for His servant, and when Moses lost his temper and acted in a way that did not bring honor to God, God dealt very harshly with him and withdrew his privilege of entering into the land.

As we mature in God, our responsibility grows, and He expects more of us. The more closely we walk with Him, the more responsible we are to walk in His will and in His way. For many others are looking to us for guidance.70

Moses knew God in a very special way. He could hear God's voice distinctly, but when he got angry and struck the rock to bring forth water, instead of simply speaking to the rock, as he had been instructed, he had to suffer the consequences (see Numbers 20:7-11).

To some, that might seem like an insignificant thing, but it wasn't insignificant to God. The rock was symbolic of Jesus. He would be crucified once, and He doesn't need us to crucify Him again and again through our rebellious acts. God demands obedience from His servants.

Because of Moses' disobedience, God raised up a new leader for the people, Joshua. Moses spoke to this new commander in the presence of all the people:

You have seen with your own eyes all that the Lord your God has done to these two kings [Sihon and Og]. The Lord will do the same to all the kingdoms over there where you are going. Do not be afraid of them; the Lord your God Himself will fight for you. Deuteronomy 3:21-22

Moses was referring to two specific earthly kings, but what about the kings in your life? What about your enemies? God has prepared victory for you over them all, as you continue to trust Him.

It doesn't matter what your problem king might

be. You owe him nothing. You belong to King Jesus and must not allow any other king to put you into bondage. You must bow only to Jesus. Say to Him, "My warrior God, please fight this enemy that's come into my life. You're stronger than any other king. Come, Lord, and fight my battle for me!" Regardless of the circumstances of your life, God is greater. He is able and willing to come to your aid. Reach out to Him in faith today and let Him fight your battles.

You belong to the King of kings and the Lord of lords, and must not serve another. Moses declared:

> *But be assured today that the Lord your God is the one who goes across ahead of you like a devouring fire. He will destroy them; He will subdue them before you.* Deuteronomy 9:3

God's favor upon the sons of Israel was not given because of their goodness. In fact, the children of Israel were often characterized by Moses as *"stiffnecked"*—meaning "stubborn or opinionated." God's favor upon them was because of His goodness. And He does not bless you because you are "good Christians," or because you attend church regularly, or because you pray, or read the Bible, or pay your tithes. God blesses you because He loves you, and nothing can change His love for us all. NOTHING!

CHAPTER SIX

BE STRONG IN THE LORD — IT'S *HIS* MIGHT

Be strong in the Lord and in His mighty power.
Ephesians 6:10

Our covenant God is on our side, and He fights for us, but that doesn't mean that He wants us to remain helpless babes for the rest of our lives, totally dependant upon His care. He wants us to mature spiritually, so He offers us the privilege of participation with Him in the battle for right.

As part of the process of maturing, God sometimes seems to leave us to face certain difficulties and to fight through them to victory, seemingly on our own. We never have to fight in our own strength, however. Although we become participants in the battle, the ultimate victory is still His. We battle *"in His mighty power."*

One of the most popular themes of our day is spiritual warfare, but spiritual warfare doesn't mean that we are left alone to fight our own battles. It means that we war alongside our God, listening to His leading as we fight, through our praises and trust, on behalf of the Church and on behalf of the purposes of God. If we work with Him, we cannot lose; for we are on the winning side.

To accomplish God's purposes, we must not only become strong in the Lord, we must become wise in the Lord — wise to His ways and His thoughts. Jesus said:

> *Behold, I send you forth as sheep in the midst of wolves: be ye therefore wise as serpents, and harmless as doves.*   Matthew 10:16, KJV

What does it mean to be as *"wise as serpents"*? In Genesis 3:1, we read that the serpent was *"subtle"* (KJV) or *"crafty"* (NIV). The word *subtle* means "analytical, skillful, ingenious, crafty, insightful, quick-witted." We are to have "a deep, searching understanding and intelligence combined with sound judgment."

I personally believe that becoming subtle (wise and skillful) believers is more important than ever before because we are living in the end time and are coming closer and closer to the Day of the Lord, the time of Christ's return; therefore God is preparing us for that unique time in history.

Just as any business looks for shrewd people to employ to further its economic purposes, God is searching for people to whom He can entrust His divine and eternal purposes for these last days.

In the Parable of the Good Steward, Jesus spoke of a man who had been hired to manage the affairs of another. In the end, the manager was accused of *"wasting his [master's] possessions"* and was called to give an account of his actions:

> *So he called him in and asked him, "What is this I hear about you? Give an account of your management, because you cannot be manager any longer."* Luke 16:2

The manager was greatly troubled at the thought of losing his job, for he had no idea how he would go on supporting himself; so he devised a plan. He would ingratiate himself with those who were indebted to his master. Then he would be welcomed into their homes if he did lose his job — which seemed inevitable at that point.

Using the authority that had not yet been stripped from him, he called each of the debtors and, when they had come, he greatly reduced the amount of the debt each one owed.

The ending phrase of this parable has often been misunderstood. Jesus said:

> *The master commended the dishonest manager because he had acted shrewdly.*   Luke 16:8

He certainly couldn't mean that the man was commended for being dishonest. In fact, the passage concludes that the man was commended *"because he had acted shrewdly."* Dishonesty is not a virtue, in any sense of the word, but men and women of shrewd, analytical thought are to be commended.

God is searching for shrewd people for His team. We have a rampaging enemy that despises anyone who is called Christian, and we cannot simply hide from him. We must take the offensive and go out to do battle for what is right. God is training His army, and, like it or not, you are part of that great force. You must prepare yourself to stand at the forefront of the battle without fear of the enemy, as you walk in reverential fear of Almighty God.

God has put some awesome weapons at our disposal. We must learn to know our weapons and to use them wisely:

> *The weapons we fight with are not the weapons of the world. On the contrary, they have divine power to demolish strongholds. We demolish arguments and every pretension that sets itself up*

*against the knowledge of God, and we take cap-
tive every thought to make it obedient to Christ.
And we will be ready to punish every act of disobedience, once your obedience is complete.*
                                        2 Corinthians 10:4-6

Because our enemies are not flesh and blood, our
weapons cannot be those of the world. We must use
divine power to demolish the spiritual and invis-
ible strongholds of the enemy. We must *"take into
captivity every thought that sets itself up against God."*
Sometimes Satan may use people, or a company,
or a system, but more often than not our battle is
with our thoughts or imaginations. Whatever the
vessel used, the source of our conflict is with *"prin-
cipalities, and powers in high places."* With God's help,
and the cooperation of other believers, we can tear
down those high places. Therefore, let us seek to be
properly armed and outfitted.
In his letter to the church at Ephesus, the Apostle
Paul instructed the believers concerning the spiritual warfare they must undertake:

*Finally, be strong in the Lord and in His mighty
power.*   Ephesians 6:10

It is not a dynamic personality or even an abundance of money that will make a person successful
in this fight. We must learn that our strength comes

from the Lord and that we can only succeed through *"His mighty power."*

Paul continued:

> *Put on the full armor of God so that you can take your stand against the devil's schemes.*
>
> Ephesians 6:11

I know that each of us wants to be able to stand against wrong, and to accept a divine mission, an assignment from God Almighty. But to do that, we must put on the armor He has provided. And we must not underestimate the battle that lies ahead. Our enemy is very real:

> *For we wrestle not against flesh and blood, but against principalities, against powers, against the rulers of the darkness of this world, against spiritual wickedness in high places.*
>
> Ephesians 6:12, KJV

In the Greek, this word *wrestle* paints an interesting picture. It implies two men locked in combat. Eventually the victor stands over his opponent, who is left lying defeated on the ground. The winner's hand is upon the other's neck. Praise God for the victories He gives us when we trust Him.

But victory doesn't come automatically. We must prepare for it:

Be Strong In the Lord — It's *His* Might

Therefore put on the full armor of God, so that when the day of evil comes, you may be able to stand your ground, and after you have done everything, to stand.   Ephesians 6:13

"After you have done everything": A more literal translation of this phrase would be "having overcome all." We are destined to "overcome all" and then to *"stand."* And how are we to *"stand"*?

Stand firm then, with the belt of truth buckled around your waist, with the breastplate of righteousness in place, and with your feet fitted with the readiness that comes from the gospel of peace.   Ephesians 6:14-15

First, we must be encircled by the truth of God's Word. It is truth that will enable us to walk in authority and in victory. Therefore, we must guard our minds and fill them with His truth.

Secondly, we must shield our hearts with righteousness — not our own, but the righteousness of Christ. As we abide in Him, His righteousness protects us from *"the fiery darts of the enemy"* that seek to do us harm.

We are to have our feet *"shod with the preparation of the gospel of peace"* (KJV). In other words, we are to be ready to take action at a moment's notice, and God's Word prepares us for that action. When the truth is proclaimed, that which is not truth is revealed for what it is. So our goal is to proclaim the Gospel of Peace, the eternal Word of the Prince of Peace.

There is more:

> *In addition to all this, take up the shield of faith, with which you can extinguish all the flaming arrows of the evil one.*   Ephesians 6:16

One of the most important pieces of our armor is the shield of faith. This troubles some, because they wonder where they can get more faith. Without it, we cannot please Him (Hebrews 11:6), but He doesn't expect us to conjure it up on our own. Faith is a gift from the Lord (Ephesians 2:8). When Christ dwells within us, faith is there. We, however, must nurture the faith God gives us and allow it to mature. The Scriptures are clear on how this is to be accomplished:

> *Faith cometh by hearing, and hearing by the word of God.*   Romans 10:17, KJV

You must feed your faith on the Word of God, and the more you feed your faith, the more it will grow. Don't make the mistake of thinking that it happens only by hearing or only by reading. It is much more than that. Your faith matures as you walk out what you read and the truths you have heard others declare. Faith grows through experiences that affirm the faithfulness of God.

The Greek word used in Ephesians 6:6 for *the shield of faith* refers to a shield the size of a door. This is no small shield behind which we must cower for protection. God is so lavish in His love and care for us that we will always be completely covered and protected when we walk in faith. When you have your shield of faith in place, you will be able to quench *"all the fiery darts"* of the evil one.

What are these *"fiery darts"* we have been referring to? They are the callous words and actions of people whom Satan uses against us. The promise of God is that if we take hold of our shield, allowing our faith to grow by immersing ourselves in the Word, those fiery darts will be put out. What a great promise!

When the enemy shoots his fiery darts at us, using the mouths and the hands of the wicked, the fire will be put out, and those darts will have no harmful effect on us.

That is not to say that no fiery darts will hit us. They may still hit us, but if we are using our shield of faith, they will not set us on fire. They will not destroy us, as the enemy intends them to.

The tongue is so powerful. James declared:

The tongue is a small part of the body, but it makes

*great boasts. Consider what a great forest is set
on fire by a small spark. The tongue also is a fire,
a world of evil among the parts of the body. It cor-
rupts the whole person, sets the whole course of
his life on fire, and is itself set on fire by hell. ...
no man can tame the tongue.*   James 3:5-7

Fiery darts that go forth with the power of the
tongue can be difficult to face. We all get hurt by
them from time to time, some more than others. Yet,
God's promise is that we don't have to be harmed
by them at all.

The Psalmist cried out for deliverance from *"lying lips"* and from *"deceitful tongues"* and firmly believed that God would come to his rescue:

*Save me, O Lord, from lying lips and from deceit-
ful tongues.
What will He do to you, and what more besides,
O deceitful tongue?
He will punish you with a warrior's sharp arrows,
with burning coals of the broom tree.*

    Psalm 120:3-4

Our God will protect us, as we faithfully prepare
ourselves for battle.

The final, and perhaps most important, part of our
protection, Paul wrote, was to:

Be Strong In the Lord — It's *His* Might

Take the helmet of salvation and the sword of the Spirit, which is the Word of God.

Ephesians 6:17

Every good soldier must keep his helmet in place. He cannot afford to leave himself vulnerable, even for a moment. We must continually walk in the process of salvation — giving God more and more say in the daily conduct of our lives, experiencing more and more of His healing, and developing more and more spiritual maturity. It is possible to be born again in a moment of time, but working out our salvation—learning to walk fully in all that God has provided for us—is a lifelong process.

Continue to work out your salvation with fear and trembling. Philippians 2:12

When every other piece of armor is in place, we must then take up the Sword of the Spirit, which, Paul said, was *"the Word of God."* What do we know about this Sword?

For the word of God is living and active. Sharper than any double-edged sword, it penetrates even to dividing soul and spirit, joints and marrow; it judges the thoughts and attitudes of the heart.

Hebrews 4:12

A good sword has two edges, and the Word of God is no exception. The Bible presents an amazing balance of truths, and that balance is important. When a person becomes fixed on one certain aspect of the truths of the Scriptures, he often becomes unbalanced in his approach to the Christian life.

As has been shown time and time again, you can take parts of the Bible and prove almost anything. When the devil came to tempt Jesus at the end of His wilderness fast, he quoted Scriptures from the Psalms, tempting Jesus to do things that would limit His effectiveness or destroy His life altogether. Jesus responded to the devil, *"But it is also written ... ,"* and He quoted from the book of Deuteronomy a passage that showed the misuse of the truth Satan had quoted.

It is so important to know both sides of what God's Word says. Anything less can cause division in the Body and confusion in your own mind and in the minds of others, as well. Use both edges of the Sword.

Having laid out the armor necessary for battle, Paul then continued, teaching the Ephesians more about spiritual warfare:

And pray in the Spirit on all occasions, with all kinds of prayers and requests. With this in mind, be alert and always keep on praying for all the saints. Ephesians 6:18

Be Strong In the Lord — It's *His* Might

When we pray, we must ask God to pray through us — in the way He desires. Our prayers can often be vain or selfish or carnal. Prayer is not just repeating words over and over, day after day. Real prayer comes from the heart and is inspired of the Spirit. Real prayer feels the heart of the Father. Prayer that does not come from the heart, prayer that is not Spirit-led, can be just so much vain repetition.

God is interested in our thoughts, intents, and motives, and sometimes our words are just a smoke screen. We might be able to fool people, but we can't fool God. Talk to God sincerely, from the depths of your very soul. Forget the vain words and pray earnestly in the Spirit.

We are to be ready to take our place in battle. We have put on *"the full armor."* Our Master has provided. We are wearing *"the belt of truth"* and *"the breastplate of righteousness."* We have our feet *"shod with the readiness of the gospel of peace."* We have *"the shield of faith"* in place, along with *"the helmet of salvation."* We have taken up *"the sword of the Spirit,"* and we are marching forward into battle, praying as we go that He will guide our every step. And we are assured of victory.

Remember, it is the power of His might that accomplishes through us what would be impossible if we tried to go it alone.

CHAPTER SEVEN

FASTING — A POWERFUL WEAPON

Is this not the kind of fasting I have chosen ... ?
Isaiah 58:6

Although we have already mentioned the fast decreed by King Jehoshaphat, this subject merits additional space here, for fasting is one of our most powerful weapons and prepares us to accept the challenge of our Lord to stand with Him in battle.

Moses fasted. The prophets, among them — Elijah, Ezra, Daniel and Anna — all fasted. King David fasted. The Apostle Paul fasted. Even Jesus Himself fasted. And that is just a partial list. Many more of the Bible characters are known to have practiced this very godly custom. And with good reason — fasting is powerful.

The people of Isaiah's day apparently didn't understand fasting any better than many believers do today. Isaiah felt compelled to give a discourse on the subject, a discourse which we find in chapter 58.

As the chapter opens, we find the people of Isaiah's day crying out to God, and asking:

> *Why have we fasted ...*
> *and you have not seen it?*
> *Why have we humbled ourselves,*
> *And you have not noticed?*   Verse 3

That seems like a fair question, and God gave them a fair answer. Their fast was not acceptable to Him. There is a right way and a wrong way to fast. God knew the hearts of those who fasted and saw that their fast was for selfish ends and their hunger led to quarrelling and even fist fights, rather than to righteousness.

It is possible to fast with impure motives. Some do it only to be seen by others and to be perceived as "holy" or "spiritual." This is unacceptable to God. He declared:

> *You cannot fast as you do today*
> *And expect your voice to be heard on high.*
>   Verse 4

What does God consider to be an acceptable fast?

> *Is this not the kind of fasting I have chosen:*
> *to loose the chains of injustice*
> *and untie the cords of the yoke,*

to set the oppressed free
and break every yoke?
Is it not to share your food with the hungry
and to provide the poor wanderer with shelter —
when you see the naked, to clothe him,
and not to turn away from your own flesh and
blood?   Isaiah 58:6-7

We must get our priorities right, or our fasting is in vain.

First of all, the purpose of fasting is not to impress anyone or to score points with God. It is to deny, for a period of time, our physical desires so that we can be more fully attuned to the spiritual realm. When we fast, we seem to shift the balance more to the spiritual side of our existence, and that allows God's Spirit greater control of our lives.

As human beings, our carnal nature is at *"enmity"* with God. It is His enemy. Each of us has a strong self-will, and our greatest priority is often to gratify our own flesh. When we decide that we want to please God more than we want to please ourselves, then we are on the right course. This self-denial results in our prayers being answered more quickly. We see the chains of injustice broken and those we minister to are set free.

Many think that if they fast they will become weak, and, in a physical sense, that may be true for a short period of time. But fasting brings to us a greater spiritual strength because in our weakness we lean on the Lord to supply the energy usually gained from the food we eat.

Fasting brings us into a higher anointing so that we can do the work of God and help to set His people free. We have a lot of work to do. We must feed those who are hungry, clothe those who are naked, and give shelter to those who are homeless. This is not just a physical feeding, clothing, and sheltering. It goes much deeper than that. We need to learn to feed people spiritually, by breaking the bread of the Word for them. We must help them be clothed with the righteousness of Jesus Christ, and we must bring them into the House of God so that they can be spiritually sheltered. Everyone needs fellowship.

Getting our priorities straight brings results to us, personally, as well as in our ministries. Remember, we are all to be ministers of God's love. Don't ever think you have no "ministry" simply because no one calls you pastor or evangelist or deacon:

> *Then your light will break forth like the dawn,*
> *and your healing will quickly appear;*
> *then your righteousness will go before you,*
> *and the glory of the Lord will be your rear guard.*
> *Then you will call, and the Lord will answer;*
> *you will cry for help, and He will say,*
> *"Here am I."*   Isaiah 58:8-9

Fasting — A Powerful Weapon

If we learn the importance of fasting and learn to discipline ourselves to fast, we can walk in light when others are walking in darkness. We can receive healing more quickly; and the righteousness of God will lead us, while the glory of God goes behind us as a rear guard. We don't have to be afraid of anything that people may say or do behind our backs. God is our Great Protector.

The glory cloud that accompanied the people of Israel during the Exodus went before them to lead them and also sat between them and their enemies, to protect them. That is exactly what God does for us when we seek Him faithfully.

There is more:

> *If you do away with the yoke of oppression,*
> *with the pointing finger and malicious talk,*
> *and if you spend yourselves in behalf of the hungry*
> *and satisfy the needs of the oppressed,*
> *then your light will rise in the darkness,*
> *and your night will become like the noonday.*
>
> Isaiah 58:9-10

We are to put away *"the yoke of oppression."* Instead of imposing ourselves and our own wishes on others, we need to relieve them of their oppression. Stop imposing your expectations on others. That is a yoke they don't need.

Years ago, I so much wanted my children and my husband to come closer to God that I sometimes tried to force them to conform to my concept of what they should be. And, as I can be stubborn when I want to be, I sometimes made their lives miserable.

This continued until one day I was able to hear the Lord say, "Carol, let go of them. You're trying to conform them to *your* image. Let Me conform them to *Mine*." That day I removed the yoke I had unwittingly placed on them and let God do His work in their lives. That worked out so much better!

Stop insisting that others live up to your expectations for them. Let the Holy Spirit deal with each individual and place the pleasant yoke of Jesus on them (Matthew 11:30).

We are also to lay aside *"malicious talk."* Other translations of this phrase include "vanity" and "insincerity." Christians must step away from hypocrisy and start *"speaking the truth in love."*

If we are willing to lay aside these things and to minister as the Scriptures direct, our *"light will rise in darkness"* and our *"night will become like the noonday."* We don't have to walk in the darkness the world walks in. We can walk in the light of Jesus Christ, who is *"the Light of the World."* His light is dwelling within you, and when you are living according to God's will and fasting in a way that pleases Him, He will *"rise"* within you:

Fasting — A Powerful Weapon

*Arise, shine, for your light has come, and the glory
of the Lord rises upon you.*   Isaiah 60:1

Isaiah goes on to say, in chapter 58:

*The Lord will guide you always;
he will satisfy your needs in a sun-scorched land
and will strengthen your frame.
You will be like a well-watered garden,
like a spring whose waters never fail.*   Verse 11

These are wonderful promises that accompany the acceptable fast. God will satisfy you and will provide for you, even in times of drought. That may be hard for some to believe, but God is faithful.

As we were growing up in Texas and Arkansas, our family was poor, and there were times when we had little or no food. Dad and Mom worked hard, but they were not always able to find work. Also, they were not practicing Christians at the time. Yet God knew that we would one day serve Him and somehow He always provided for us. Sometimes His provision came as my mother sent my younger sisters into the woods behind our house to gather greens. Sometimes it came through financial assistance from the government. Sometimes it came through a friend who just "happened" to drop by with extra food. I have seen it happen so many times that I know that God provides for His own, even before they know Him as Lord.

The King James version renders the phrase *"and will strengthen your frame"* as *"and [shall] make fat thy bones."* While this specifically implies that we will have healthy bones, a wider implication is that He will make us physically strong.

The spiritual blessing is there too, in the *"well-watered garden"* and the *"spring whose waters never fail."* Oh, that the Church today would be made up of those *"whose waters never fail,"* that we would always be ready to give others a drink of living water! I want to be so filled with the Word of God and the Spirit of God that people can come to me and receive a drink any time of the night or day. That is what I believe God wants for all His people.

The blessings of fasting even pass to the next generations:

> *Your people will rebuild the ancient ruins*
> *and will raise up the age-old foundations;*
> *you will be called Repairer of Broken Walls,*
> *Restorer of Streets with Dwellings.*   Verse 12

When you seek God as He requires of you, the members of your family are destined to become productive citizens. They shall be renowned as *"the repairer[s] of the breech, the restorer[s] of paths to dwell in"* (KJV). Your children can inherit your blessing, so if you want your children to be those who restore and not those who tear down, if you want them to be known as repairers and not as wreckers, then you must set the example for them now and train them in the ways of God for their own future.

Another of the positive results of fasting which was mentioned by Isaiah and which is emphasized throughout scripture is that fasting brings humility. Nothing could be more important to our spiritual welfare. Jesus said:

> *For whoever exalts himself will be humbled, and whoever humbles himself will be exalted.*
>
> Matthew 23:12

Fasting, in this sense, is a privilege, for which we should all be grateful. It's not comfortable, but it is rewarding.

Twice Israel was defeated by the little tribe of Benjamin. It happened because Israel, so much larger than Benjamin, was overconfident. But when the people of Israel humbled themselves with fasting, God came to their aid and Benjamin was defeated. Fasting is a powerful tool which produces humility in those who practice it.

One of the more familiar fasts of the Old Testament is that of Daniel and his three Hebrew friends, Hananiah, Mishael, and Azariah (later renamed by the Babylonians as Shadrach, Meshach and Abednego). The four of them had been chosen among the captive Hebrews in Babylon to be trained for the service of the king. Part of that training included a provision of food from the king's table—quite an honor.

Daniel and his friends, however, determined to please God in all things. So, despite the urgings of the official in charge of the captive trainees, the four received permission to eat only vegetables for ten days. Everyone was sure that this would cause them to lose out in the competitive environment of the palace training grounds.

At the end of the ten days, an amazing discovery was made. The four Hebrew children, eating their simple and sacrificial diet, were visibly healthier than any of the other young men in their training class. God had honored their fast and their obedience to the dietary laws of their people.

Quite a different type of fast is described in Daniel chapter 10:

> *At that time I, Daniel, mourned for three weeks. I ate no choice food; no meat or wine touched my lips; and I used no lotions at all until the three weeks were over.*   Daniel 10:2-3

This word *mourn* is used frequently throughout the Old Testament in the context of fasting, and seems to denote a seriousness and dedication to a divine purpose. During this fast, Daniel ate only simple fare. His attitude seems to have been, "Lord, I want to please You more that I want to seek my own comfort." So he *"ate no choice food,"* or as the King James Version relates, *"no pleasant bread."*

Job had the same attitude:

> *I have not departed from the commands of his lips;*
> *I have treasured the words of his mouth more than*
> *my daily bread.* Job 23:12

As Daniel was earnestly seeking the Lord, he had a vision. In the vision, he saw an angelic being who had come to him with a message from God. Others, who were with him at the time, were frightened by a great quaking, and had run to hide somewhere, so Daniel was the only one who saw the angel and received the word of the Lord. The angel said:

> *Do not be afraid, Daniel. Since the first day that*
> *you set your mind to gain understanding and to*
> *humble yourself before your God, your words were*
> *heard, and I have come in response to them. But*
> *the prince of the Persian kingdom resisted me*
> *twenty-one days.* Daniel 10:12-13

"Twenty-one days" ... That was exactly the period Daniel had fasted. It was only at the end of the twenty-one days that this angelic being was allowed to break through the opposition to bring Daniel his

answer. This is the power which fasting unleashes in the heavenlies.

Many of us have yet to realize the power our prayer and fasting have in the heavenly realm, and we surely need much more teaching on this subject in the days ahead.

There are so many other fasts recorded in the Bible that space would not permit us to mention them all, but a few cannot be omitted.

One of the instances I find quite remarkable occurred when the prophet Jonah finally obeyed God and went to Nineveh to preach. The results were astonishing. The heathen king of that place responded to the Word of the Lord by calling for a three-day fast from all food and all water. Even the animals were not allowed food or drink. As a result of that fast (and because of the repentant spirit it represented), Nineveh was spared from the wrath of God.

Ezra the scribe, when he led the people of Israel out of captivity in the land of Babylon, had told the Babylonian king that God would protect the people, giving them a safe journey back to Jerusalem. After boasting of God's power in this way, he was ashamed to ask for troops to protect his people as they went on their way. Instead, he called the people to fast, and God answered their prayer (see Ezra 8) and saw them home in victory.

Queen Esther fasted and called others to fast with her, during a time of crisis for her people. The Book of Esther shows how God used that prayer and fasting to bring about the salvation of the entire nation.

Early Christians clearly believed that fasting was not just for Old Testament times. Many of them fasted two days a week. This tradition was carried over into many of the revival movements of later centuries. It is said that John Wesley refused to ordain any man and set him into a place of ministry in the Methodist movement unless that man first agreed to fast two days each week until the evening meal.

We all need to learn to use *"the weapons of our warfare,"* fasting included. It is not nearly as difficult as many have made it seem. Most people can fast — if they do it in the right way. The key is to let the Lord lead you. If He leads you, He will be there to help you when you need His help.

It is best, I have found, to begin your habit of fasting slowly, a little at a time. Too many people have attempted long fasts without first establishing the discipline necessary to carrying such a fast to its conclusion.

I personally know many people who have fasted forty days, and some do it on a yearly basis. Most of those people, however, don't fast that long without daily taking some form of liquid, usually fruit juices or puree, in addition to water.

Be led of the Spirit of God. Do your fast in God's time and in His way, and you will have success, and you won't die. You can live for a few days without natural food, as Jesus said:

> *It is written, 'Man does not live on bread alone, but on every word that comes from the mouth of God.'* Matthew 4:4

> *My food ... is to do the will of Him who sent Me and to finish His work.* John 4:34

As you learn to fast, you will unleash the power of this weapon, one that will give you many victories in the heavenly places in the years to come, victories that will be made manifest here on earth in everyday situations.

CHAPTER EIGHT

THE BLESSING OF THE LORD — HOW FULFILLING!

The blessing of the Lord brings wealth, and He adds no trouble to it. Proverbs 10:22

Because we are God's children and inextricably joined to Him in covenant, we are entitled to His blessing. The blessing of God is a biblical concept that seems simple, yet isn't nearly as simple as it seems. One dictionary defines *blessing* as "something promoting or contributing to happiness; something contributing to our well-being or prosperity." This is probably the definition that most often comes to mind when we think of the word, but the Hebrew word translated *blessing* goes much further.

It is not uncommon for us to misunderstand what the Bible says. We may think we are familiar with a biblical term, but barriers of culture and language stand in our way and often cause us not to see clearly what God is trying to say to His people.

The Hebrew term for *blessing* conveyed the meaning: "May the power of God come upon you. May an envelope or tent of His power and His protection surround you. May His enabling power give you success and prosperity in everything you do. May you reach your full potential in God. In all you touch, may you have that prosperity and success that God desires you to have; so much so that you will be able to bless others because you have abundance of prosperity, nonmaterial as well as material, coming through victoriously in every situation of life." That's true wealth, and God's desire for each of us!

Many of the wealthy of our world have made their fortunes in ways that did not bring glory to God, and they have to live with that knowledge. Too often, along with their wealth, has come great sorrow and great disquiet. Consequently, many wealthy people are emotionally troubled.

God wants His people to have peace in the midst of prosperity, a peace that is so noticeable that others cannot help but see that we are different. That is not to say that we won't face many of the same problems that others face. In fact, the Scriptures declare:

Many are the afflictions of the righteous.
Psalm 34:19

The Blessing of the Lord — How Fulfilling!

Thank God the verse does not end with that declaration. It contains a wonderful promise:

> ... *but the Lord delivers him out of them all.*
>
> Psalm 34:19

Are those two thoughts contradictory? Not really. Sometimes blessing comes in disguise. When Joseph was imprisoned in Egypt, not many would have looked at his situation and said, "That man is truly blessed of God." Yet we know that his unjust imprisonment and his godly conduct in prison did lead to his being selected as the prime minister of Egypt and brought about the saving of the Hebrew race.

When David was being pursued by the demented King Saul, who would have said, "Oh, David is so blessed of God to have to flee for his life in that way"? Yet God was working out something wonderful in David that prepared him to be king in Saul's stead.

Often what God calls a blessing, what He uses as His means of bringing us into conformity to the image of His Son, might even seem like a curse to us. We get upset about it, wondering why this thing is happening. Has God forgotten us? Have we lost His favor? Are we separated from His love?

When our confidence in the goodness of our heavenly Father reaches the necessary level that we understand His promise that *"all things work together*

for good to them that love God," we can learn to thank
Him in the midst of difficult situations. We can say,
"Thank You, Lord! Regardless of the circumstances,
I know that You are working for my good and that I
will be blessed."

We don't thank God because we are hurting or
because we are in situations that bring us pain. We
thank Him because we know that in His great love
for us, He would not allow these things to be happening unless He intended to make them work together for our good, for His good, and for the good
of the Kingdom of God. This is a wonderfully comforting thought:

> *And we know that in all things God works for the
> good of those who love Him, who have been called
> according to His purpose.*   Romans 8:28

God's ultimate intention is that we might be conformed to the image of His Son, and He will use
whatever means necessary to bring us to that place.
So, whatever happens, it is for our good.

A very similar promise that is often misunderstood and under-appreciated is that God will give
us the *"desires of [our] hearts"*:

> *Delight yourself in the Lord and He will give you
> the desires of your heart.*   Psalm 37:4

The Blessing of the Lord — How Fulfilling!

The Hebrew word *anag*, here translated *delight yourself* [to delight in] means "to become pliable in the hands of God." Some people think they *are* delighting in God and wonder why He has not yet given them the desires of their heart. They may be misunderstanding the promise. Are you pliable in His hands? Have you allowed His fires to melt you to the point that He can mold you as He desires?

Loving the Lord is one thing, but letting Him put us into the fire to remold and reshape us is something else entirely, something that most of us run from. But we shouldn't. God's fire is not meant to destroy us. Its purpose is to bring to the surface the impurities in our lives — the dross — so that He can skim it off, as a refiner who works with fine metals. His desire is to see us become pure gold.

Some of the fires we face may be very hot, but they will not cause us harm, if our eyes are fixed on Him. Yield to the fire, and allow it to make you soft and pliable in the hands of God. That is what it means to *"delight in the Lord."*

How is it that God can promise us *"the desires of [our] heart"*? It is because, when we have gone through the fires, our hearts are purified and God can trust that what we want is what He wants for us, as well.

The thought of this verse continues into the next:

Commit your way to the Lord; trust in Him and He will do this.   Psalm 37:5

The Hebrew phrase, here translated, *"commit your way to the Lord"* means "to roll all your cares onto the Lord." The next verse tells us what will happen when we learn to do this:

He will make your righteousness shine like the dawn, the justice of your cause like the noonday sun. Psalm 37:6

What a great promise!

Let's take a closer look at Joseph's situation. It is a perfect example for us to emulate. Joseph was a man who was truly blessed of God, and who knew that he was blessed, but many of his blessings appeared to be greatly disguised for a time. The fact that they were indeed blessings was not immediately apparent.

Joseph's brothers sold him into slavery during his teenage years. The only thing he had done to deserve such cruel treatment was to report to his father when his brothers weren't doing their jobs properly. Joseph was a conscientious young man.

It is possible that he had flaunted the beautiful coat his father gave him, and the fact that the coat was a visible reminder that he was Jacob's favorite son didn't help either. Joseph may not have used wisdom when he told his brothers, too eagerly perhaps, that he had seen them bowing down to him in a dream. Lack of wisdom and tact would not be unusual for a lad of his age. But slavery?

The Blessing of the Lord — How Fulfilling!

For whatever external reasons, God allowed Joseph to start his special training on this low note, a training that would last for some twenty years. The camel caravan that bought him that day took him to Egypt and auctioned him off to the highest bidder. Before long, he was face-to-face with his new master, an Egyptian military captain named Potiphar. What happened to Joseph in the house of Potiphar should also be true of us wherever we happen to find ourselves:

> *Joseph found favor in his eyes and became his attendant. Potiphar put him in charge of his household, and he entrusted to his care everything he owned. From the time he put him in charge of his household and of all that he owned, the Lord blessed the household of the Egyptian because of Joseph. The blessing of the Lord was on everything Potiphar had, both in the house and in the field.*
>
> Genesis 39:4-5

Potiphar became blessed because Joseph was blessed, and Joseph was in his household — despite the fact that he was a slave.

This is what God intends for all of His people. If you are a born-again child of God, He not only wants to bless you, but He wants to bless everyone around you. You are blessed so that you can become a blessing to others. You are an extension of Christ on the earth. He is the Light of the World, and has called us to be the light in our dark world (see Matthew 5:14).

Start shining — wherever you are. Start shining — whatever your circumstances. Start shining — no matter how hot the fire.

Joseph did not curse Potiphar because he found himself enslaved to the man. He became a blessing to him, instead. What a wonderful example for each of us!

When Potiphar's wife took a personal liking to Joseph and began pursuing him, trying to seduce him, Joseph resisted. One day, when she insisted rather strongly and took hold of Joseph's garment, he left it in her hands and fled. Spurned, the woman turned on Joseph and reported to her husband that Joseph had tried to molest her. In her hand, she held the proof: his cloak. Joseph was immediately sent to prison.

Prison might have signified the end for Joseph. It destroys many men, but it was not to be so in Joseph's case:

> *But while Joseph was there in prison, the Lord was with him; he showed him kindness and granted him favor in the eyes of the prison warden. So the warden put Joseph in charge of all those held in the prison, and he was made responsible for all that was done there. The warden paid no*

The Blessing of the Lord — How Fulfilling!

*attention to anything under Joseph's care, because
the Lord was with Joseph and gave him success
in whatever he did.* Genesis 39:20-23

The warden of the prison was blessed because Joseph was blessed, and that's exactly what God wants. Joseph was not meant to curse the warden and his fellow inmates, just because he had been wronged. He was wronged and sent to prison so that he could bless these people. In the meantime, as one Bible translation puts it, *"iron was worked in his soul,"* while he was imprisoned (Psalm 105:19).

Joseph could have been discouraged when years went by and his wrongful imprisonment was not discovered, but he wasn't. He might have given up when a servant of the king, whom he had befriended and helped, promised to put a good word in to the king on his behalf but forgot. But Joseph knew God, and he knew that whatever God was doing would ultimately end in his favor, so he was patient and faithful, through every fiery trial that came his way.

In the end, the Lord worked powerfully through Joseph to save many lives. His gift of being able to interpret the dreams of others not only blessed those around him but brought him fame and power. Because he correctly interpreted the Pharaoh's dream, he moved from the prison to the palace and became the second in command in the Egyptian Empire. And

109

in the coming years, the Pharaoh prospered because of the blessing that was upon Joseph.

As second in command, Joseph controlled the movement of grains during the years of plenty he had foreseen, and was able, through that position, to reconcile with his entire family. As a result, all Israel was blessed, because Joseph was blessed. That's what God wants for you, as well — for you to be a blessing to others.

Could being thrown into a fiery furnace be a blessing? Yes!

When the people of Israel, many years later, were taken captive to Babylon, Nebuchadnezzar, the pagan king, built a huge statue of gold, ninety feet tall, and commanded that everyone bow down before it whenever certain instruments were played. At least three Hebrew men, men who had learned to delight in God and were not about to bow down to some pagan god, refused to comply. They were the famous trio: Shadrach, Meshach, and Abednego.

Something unusual had already been noted in the lives of these three men, and, as a result, they had been given authority over certain sectors of Babylon. Perhaps because of this unusual authority that had been vested in them as slaves, their reaction to the king's command was closely watched. When it was noted that they chose not to bow down to Nebuchadnezzar's image, a group of men who were extremely jealous of the position of the three reported the matter to the king.

The Blessing of the Lord — How Fulfilling!

Nebuchadnezzar was enraged by this flagrant disregard of his orders and the lack of gratitude on the part of slaves who had been elevated beyond their normal possibility, so he called for the men to be brought at once. He did not pronounce an immediate sentence upon the men, for somehow he liked them and wanted to keep them in their place. He decided to give them one more chance. They simply could not disobey him, he made them to understand. They would either bow before the statue when the celebratory music was played, or they would be cast into a blazing furnace.

The response of the three men to this threat has utterly amazed Bible readers down through the centuries. Did they have a choice? They thought so, and they made their choice, without hesitation:

O Nebuchadnezzar, we do not need to defend ourselves before you in this matter. If we are thrown into the blazing furnace, the God we serve is able to save us from it, and He will rescue us from your hand, O king. But even if He does not, we want you to know, O king, that we will not serve your gods or worship the image of gold that you have set up. Daniel 3:16-17

You may be wondering how you would have reacted in a similar situation, and I certainly have to wonder what I would have done. Are we ready to take such a stand? Are we ready to rise up and be the man or woman that God has called us to be?

Fear is a paralyzing force, and our heavenly Father wants us to be so delighted in Him and in His promises to us that we will have no fear of what men can do to us.

The three Hebrew children seemed utterly helpless in this situation, yet they knew that God was in control and that He would back them up if they were willing to take a stand for Him. If they had to face the fiery furnace, then God had a purpose for it, and they were ready for that. If they died, they would still come out ahead. So, what did they have to lose? What are we afraid of? God is on our side. We also cannot lose — if we follow Him faithfully.

When Nebuchadnezzar heard the reply the three men gave, he was absolutely furious. These men were beyond saving and must be made an example of. He ordered the furnace to be heated seven times hotter than usual:

> *[The king] commanded some of the strongest soldiers in his army to tie up Shadrach, Meshach and Abednego and throw them into the blazing furnace. So these men ... were bound and thrown into the blazing furnace. The king's command was so urgent and the furnace so hot that the flames of the fire killed the soldiers who took up Shadrach, Meshach and Abednego ... .* Daniel 3:20-23

The Blessing of the Lord — How Fulfilling!

What a terrible fire! Just getting near it was deadly, let alone being thrown into the midst of it. The soldiers who threw the Hebrews into the fire were killed by the intensity of its heat.

Be careful that you don't ask someone else to go into a fire that was meant for you. They might not survive. You may not have the grace to go through what God is allowing someone else to experience right now. Let each of us face his own fire and trust God for the grace to survive it. Leave all those decisions with God. He knows what He is doing.

It wouldn't have done the Hebrew children any good to become angry and rail against Nebuchadnezzar or against the men that bound them. These were just agents of God, and if God puts you into the fire, don't take your wrath out on those who bind you and throw you in. Leave them with God.

Many times we are locked into circumstances we can't control, bound by something that we can't understand. What should we do in those moments? Instead of taking our frustrations out on others, we need to turn our faces toward Jesus, cry out to Him and watch, as He comes to our aid. This is exactly the response that saved the three Hebrews, but if they had vented their frustration instead, they might have missed the grace of God for their coming trial.

Nebuchadnezzar apparently sat back to watch, in satisfaction, the destruction of those "rebellious slaves." Then, suddenly he was on his feet, and there was an amazed expression on his face, as he called to others nearby:

> *"Weren't there three men that we tied up and threw into the fire?" They replied, "Certainly, O king." He said, "Look! I see four men walking around in the fire, unbound and unharmed, and the fourth looks like a son of the gods."*
>
> Daniel 3:24-25

We can only imagine Nebuchadnezzar's excitement. Three men had been cast in, but now there were four men, and they were *"unbound"* and *"unharmed"* and *"the fourth look[ed] like a son of the gods."* The King James Version renders this phrase as: *"the fourth is like the son of God."* That was amazing.

Nebuchadnezzar called to the three men and told them to come out of the furnace. When they obeyed, we can only imagine the noisy scene. All of the king's advisors, the governor, and all of those who were in positions of authority immediately crowded around the men, looking at them, examining them, asking them excited questions. They were not able to detect any harm to the men's bodies. Even their hair was not singed. Their robes were not scorched, and there was no smell of smoke upon them. How could that be?

Having witnessed that convincing display, it didn't take Nebuchadnezzar long to decide that he wanted to praise *"the God of Shadrach, Meshach, and Abednego."* He decreed that same day that no one should be allowed to speak against this God, and he proceeded to promote the three men who had demonstrated God's grace so convincingly.

You may be facing your fiery furnace today. If so, I urge you to call upon the Lord God Almighty. Say to Him, "Lord, come and walk with me in this fire," and He will do it. He is eager to hear your cry and will bring you forth — *"unbound and unharmed,"* a testimony to His goodness.

When difficulty comes to our lives, it is always easier to give up than to press ahead. But God is counting on us, as mature believers, to take a stand against the kingdoms of this world and to take back that which lawfully belongs to our God and His people. We must persevere until we see the promised blessing.

The Psalmist knew what it was to go through fire:

> *You let men ride over our heads; we went through fire and water, but You brought us to a place of abundance.*   Psalm 66:12

Psalm 66, in general, is a psalm of praise to God, yet right in the middle of the praise, the psalmist pauses to remember some of the trials the Israelites endured when leaving Egypt and traveling toward the Promised Land.

The end result of the trials they faced, he shows, was that they were *"brought ... to a place of abundance."* The King James Version translates that phrase as, *"a place of rich fulfillment."* The Hebrew word used here is *revawyah* and means "to satisfy the appetite." God was bringing His people to a place where they would be totally satisfied. But, along the way, they had to face certain trials.

"You let men ride over our heads; we went through fire and water," the psalmist remembers, *"but ..."* And what followed the *"but"* was glorious. God brought His people to a place of abundant blessing.

This word *revawyah* is used only one other time in the Old Testament, in Psalm 23, when David wrote, *"My cup overflows"* (verse 5). This is the end result of facing the trials of life and remaining strong in our faith in God. Overflowing blessings await us.

After Israel had come into her inheritance in Canaan, before any king had been chosen to lead the people, they were under judges, men and women whom God raised up to make wise decisions for His people. These were champions in faith, and Israel needed champions, for they had many enemies.

One of Israel's judges was Gideon. As a youth, he had been considered, for some reason, *"the least of his father's household."* This may have meant that he was the youngest.

The Midianites had set up camp just north of Israel and had plundered the countryside, forcing the Israelites to go into hiding and to process what little grain they could keep to themselves in caves or other secretive locations. What a humiliating situation!

One day, as Gideon was threshing wheat in a winepress, an angel of the Lord came to him and called on him to rise up and defeat the Midianites.

Gideon was very reluctant to believe what he was hearing. Why would God choose him? His was not one of the more respected families in Israel, and he was *"the least in his father's household."* That seemed to make him the most unlikely candidate for leadership.

Through a series of signs, God confirmed His will to Gideon, and the youth eventually accepted the challenge. There's nothing wrong with wanting to be sure that we are hearing correctly from God — when we are determined to obey Him once we understand clearly His leading. When Gideon was sure of his calling, he took immediate steps to do what God was saying, and when he did, a wonderful thing happened :

> *Then the Spirit of the Lord came upon Gideon, and he blew a trumpet, summoning the Abiezrites to follow him. He sent messengers throughout Manasseh, calling them to arms, and also into Asher, Zebulun and Naphtali, so that they too went up to meet them.* Judges 6:34-35

The Amplified Version says it in a different way:

> *But the Spirit of the Lord clothed Gideon with Himself and took possession of him.*
>
> Judges 6:34, AMP

God can clothe us with Himself and take possession of us, and that assures us of victory against any enemy.

Why should we resist this? We already belong to the Lord; we have been purchased with Christ's own blood. Why not let Him possess us? Why not let Him clothe us? Why not let Him raise us up as the champions of faith that are so needed in our world today?

The battle was not to be fought in the way Gideon had imagined:

> *The Lord said to Gideon, "You have too many men for me to deliver Midian into their hands. In order that Israel may not boast against me that her own strength has saved her, announce now to the people, 'Anyone who trembles with fear may turn back and leave Mount Gilead.'" So twenty-two thousand men left, while ten thousand remained.*
>
> Judges 7:2-3

When Gideon had first blown the trumpet, calling anyone who was willing to fight, thirty-two thousand men had responded. That was not a bad start. It would not form nearly as big an army as the enemy forces had amassed, but it was better than nothing. Surely it would grow, as others took up the challenge.

But God wanted the glory of victory to be His alone, and He wanted to make sure that the men of Israel did not rely on their own strength. So He put forth a test of the volunteers and told Gideon to send home anyone who failed it. Any man who was fearful could not serve in the armies of God.

This decision was understandable. Fear is contagious and quickly infects others. Gideon didn't need any cowards in his ranks. Still, he hoped that not many would be eliminated by this test — perhaps a few hundred men, at the most, he must have imagined.

When Gideon made the public announcement that anyone who was fearful could go home, he surely was not prepared for the outcome. Twenty-two thousand men took him at his word, picked up their bundles of possessions, and ran off, quickly disappearing from sight. Gideon was suddenly reduced to ten thousand men and was wondering how he could defeat such a large host with such a few men.

Still, God was not satisfied and gave Gideon a second test to present to his volunteers. He was to take his troops to a nearby watering hole, and anyone who knelt down to drink, relaxing their guard, would be eliminated, while those who remained alert, bringing the water to their mouths with their hands and lapping it up, would form the backbone of his troops.

The thought of reducing his numbers even more must have been disheartening to Gideon, nevertheless he obeyed the Lord and took the men to the watering place. Surely not many would go home this time.

What happened next was confounding. Out of the ten thousand potential soldiers, only three hundred drank as God had directed Gideon, and all the rest had to be sent home. This could have been very discouraging for the young man, except that Gideon was hearing from the Lord every step of the way. God promised His servant:

> *"With the three hundred men that lapped I will save you and give the Midianites into your hands. Let all the other men go, each to his own place."* *So Gideon sent the rest of the Israelites to their tents but kept the three hundred, WHO TOOK OVER THE PROVISIONS AND TRUMPETS OF THE OTHERS.* Judges 7:7-8

What a turn of events! In a short period of time, Gideon went from a respectable group of thirty-two thousand warriors to a piddling few. What were three hundred men against such a host of enemies?

For those who see only in the natural realm, defeat would now seem to be assured. But this tiny army would soon show forth God's blessing on Gideon and all Israel, and would allow everyone to see that He, the Lord of Hosts, was in control.

Gideon and his small band of warriors were victorious against the Midianites, using a battle plan that only God could have devised. The three hundred men encircled the Midianite camp and used something we might call "noise and light warfare." They made so much noise and the light shining through three hundred broken vessels was so sudden that they caused the enemy to panic. The Lord brought confusion upon the Midianites, and they turned on one another. As the Midianites fled in disarray, Israel's tiny band was in hot pursuit.

Gideon's ready obedience when he was certain he had heard the Lord, and his willingness to let God fight for him brought the nation victory. But all along the way, Gideon had to be believing that everything that was happening to them was for a reason and would end in their ultimate blessing. He was right.

Don't despise or resist what God is doing in your life. He is using life's circumstances to perfect you.

There is an ultimate place of blessing, a place where we can go to receive what the Lord has for us, and to offer our all to Him. That place is the cross, the place of sacrifice, the place where Jesus made it possible for us to become sons and daughters of God, and, thus, heirs of all His goodness. To many, the cross was a curse, but we know it to have been the ultimate blessing in disguise. The men who promoted it meant it for evil, but God meant it for our good and for the salvation of the whole world.

All blessings flow from that one act, and through the sacrifice of Christ on Calvary we can now have redemption and salvation, for body, soul, and spirit. It was there, in that one supreme act of obedience, the willingness to shed His own blood, that Christ made possible our becoming covenantal partners with the Lord God.

The blessings of the cross can be ours only if we are willing to lay our own desires, wishes and agendas at the feet of the Savior. It comes only as we recognize the greatness of what He has done for us, and we learn to praise Him, even in the midst of difficulties.

His crucifixion made possible our own. Paul wrote:

> *I have been crucified with Christ and I no longer live, but Christ lives in me. The life I live in the body, I live by faith in the Son of God, who loved me and gave Himself for me.* Galatians 2:20

On that cross, Jesus bore your sins and mine. He bore the sins of every individual who has lived or will live in every generation of time. It is incomprehensible, yet He took all our afflictions, all our shame, all our embarrassment, and all our hurt. Our sins and the results of our sins were buried with Him, and when He arose from the dead, He brought us new life.

He said, "It is finished." There is nothing left to do. He has done it all. So what are we waiting for? All that remains is for us to accept and receive the benefits of the cross. They are ours for the asking.

Say to Him today: "Lord Jesus, I believe You died for me and that my sins went with You to the grave. You have already paid for them. Now, I ask You to help me to receive Your forgiveness and Your salvation."

The yielding of ourselves to Christ, to some, would seem like loss; yet, through it, we gain everything. To some, it would seem like surrender; yet, by doing it, we gain our greatest victory. To some, it would seem like total self-denial; yet, through that one simple act, we assure for ourselves a blessed life here on earth and an eternity in the presence of God.

CHAPTER NINE

TRUSTING IN HIM — EVEN IN DARKNESS

Praise the Lord! For all who fear God and trust in him are blessed beyond expression. Yes, happy is the man who delights in doing his commands. His children shall be honored everywhere, for good men's sons have a special heritage. He himself shall be wealthy, and his good deeds will never be forgotten. When darkness overtakes him, light will come bursting in. Psalm 112:1-4, TLB

Unto the upright there ariseth light in the darkness. Psalm 112:4, KJV

The fact that God is with us and is on our side does not mean that we will never face darkness. If it were not for a little darkness in our lives, we might not appreciate the light we do have.

Why Do We Struggle So?

All of us have problems at one time or another. Even mature Christians experience clouds of confusion periodically and don't know which way to turn. Very fine upright individuals often find themselves struggling under mountains of debt or facing devastating disease or divorce or runaway children.

But God has a promise for us, and it is glorious: *"Unto the upright there ariseth light in the darkness."* God has not promised to prevent troubles from being part of life's experience, but He has promised that He will be there to give us light in the midst of darkness.

Our God knows the answers to all our problems and is able to drive away confusion from our minds. He is able to resolve every debt and every marital conflict and to give us perfect victory in every dark trial — when we trust Him for it.

There are two things that we need to realize concerning why God permits serious problems. First, from His viewpoint, they are not intended to do us harm, only to test us and to show us the glory of God's light. Secondly, we are to be shining lights in the midst of this world's darkness. This can only happen as we fill up on Him who is Light and then let His presence overcome through us, piercing the darkness around us. We must remember, the Light of the world is on our side. God wants us to be free from all fear.

Trusting In Him — Even In Darkness

There can be no question that in our world we face some very serious challenges to our faith. If you dwell on the problem, you will get discouraged. Dwell on the Answer. Ask Him who is Light to rise up within you and dispel all darkness.

When you enter a darkened room, the first thing you look for is a light switch. When you find it and flip on the light, the darkness disappears, and you can see where you are going and what you are doing. Light dispels darkness, and when your light is greater than the darkness around you, that darkness will flee.

At night, when you are in a lighted room in your home, if you open the shade on a window, the darkness from outside does not rush in to envelop your room in darkness. No! The light from your room rushes out to dispel the darkness outside, and that's what God wants for each of us.

You have nothing to fear. Focus your eyes on Jesus and place your trust in Him. The Scriptures promise:

> *Thou will keep in perfect peace him whose mind is steadfast, because he trusts in You.*
> Isaiah 26:3

> *His [the righteous man's] heart is secure, he will have no fear; in the end he will look in triumph on his foes.*
> Psalm 112:8

Darkness brings fear, but God wants to establish you and give you a heart free from that fear. Probably none of us are totally free in this sense. We all suffer tinges of fear, at times. But being afraid and being "full of fear" are two different things. Admit your fear to the Lord and let Him dispel it. David readily admitted his fear:

> *When I am afraid, I will trust in You.*
>
> Psalm 56:3

As David did, allow God's bright light to arise within you and to establish you in His love. And when your heart is established in God's love, you will not be moved or shaken by the darkness around you:

> *Who is going to harm you if you are eager to do good? But even if you should suffer for what is right, you are blessed. "Do not fear what they [the unrighteous] fear; do not be frightened." But in your hearts set apart Christ as Lord. Always be prepared to give an answer to everyone who asks you to give the reason for the hope that you have. But do this with gentleness and respect.*
>
> 1 Peter 3:13-15

Other people will be watching how you go through trials. When they see you walk with confidence in the Lord instead of totally falling apart, they, too, will ask, "What's the reason for the hope you have?" What an opportunity to tell them about our God!

David's strength was knowing that God was his only hope. Even in the midst of situations that looked hopeless, he could cry out to God and find the answer he needed for the moment.

David faced many dark days during his lifetime. At one low point of his life, when Saul was pursuing him and jealously trying to kill him, David sought refuge in a Philistine camp. The Philistines were traditionally enemies of Israel, and when the Philistine king, Abimelech, questioned the presence of David in the camp, David feigned madness in order to escape the wrath of the Philistines.

What a situation! There he was in the midst of his enemies, hiding from his own king and having to disguise his very sanity in order to survive. What would you have done? Yet, in the midst of this terribly dark hour, David began to sing to the Lord:

I will extol the Lord at all times;
His praise will always be on my lips.
My soul will boast in the Lord;
let the afflicted hear and rejoice.
Glorify the Lord with me;
let us exalt His name together.

Why Do We Struggle So?

I sought the Lord, and He answered me;
He delivered me from all my fears.

Psalm 34:1-4

What a testimony! With enemies on every side, David could confidently declare that the Lord had delivered him from all his fears. This should bring hope to every one of us, for the God of David is our God, as well.

Isaiah challenged the people of God not to be afraid:

But now, this is what the Lord says —
he who created you, O Jacob,
he who formed you, O Israel:
"Fear not, for I have redeemed you;
I have summoned you by name; you are mine."

Isaiah 43:1

If you are experiencing fear that threatens to over-whelm you, know that the Lord is with you. Your covenantal Partner will never forsake you. He bought you with His own blood, a price greater than you can imagine. You belong to Him. He loves you, and He is on your side. Therefore no harm can come to you. He will deliver you through His Word. We are all hurt from time to time, but God will keep us from harm. There is a big difference in the two words.

Trusting In Him — Even In Darkness

As parents, we can understand a little how God feels about His children. When our children are hurting, we hurt too. When they are afraid, we suffer for them. We will do anything to protect them and to keep them from harm. How much more our heavenly Father cares for us!

We must learn to fear only God:

Fear of man will prove to be a snare, but whoever trusts in the Lord is kept safe.   Proverbs 29:25

The Hebrew word translated *snare* paints a picture. It is saying that man can literally put a snare, or a noose, around your neck and lead you anywhere he wants you to go. If you are fearful of what men might do to you, the Lord wants you to be free of that fear. Fear God alone, and you will prosper. He is able to make your enemies live at peace with you:

When a man's ways are pleasing to the Lord, He makes even his enemies live at peace with him.
Proverbs 16:7

Notice that there is a condition for this promise: *"When a man's ways please the Lord."* Are you in the habit of trying to please God, or are you one of those who constantly seek to please the people around you? God is looking for those who will look to Him and ask, "God, what pleases You in this situation? Father, what do You want me to do?" When you ask this question, what God shows you may not please anyone else, but if it pleases Him, that's the important thing.

When we seek to live lives that are pleasing to God, there will be times that our choices are unpopular and other people may turn against us. When this happens, don't worry about it. The One who is on our side will place great peace in our hearts in exchange for the sorrow we feel when others are displeased with our decisions.

Live to please your heavenly Father, and if you please Him, you will also please those who are His, those who are walking the same path. The goal is to please God, and nothing could be more important in life.

The fear of God, which is a deep reverence for His greatness, will bring you untold blessing. All other kinds of fear rob us. If you are consumed by fear, you will never know happiness. As long as you are dreading what the next moments might bring — the next day, or the next week — you will never know true joy. Incapacitating fear is part of the curse intended for those who resist God and should not be part of the Christian experience (Deuteronomy 28:15-68).

Jesus took our curse upon His own body as He hung upon the tree and paid our debt so that we could be free from sin and its curse. Receive the deliverance that is already provided through that sacrifice, and live free from all fear.

When I speak of fear, I do so from experience. I know what it is to be paralyzed by this sinister force. For one solid year I experienced anxiety attacks. It was a terrible experience that I wouldn't wish on anyone.

I have been free from fear now for twenty-six years because God heard my cry and came and set me free. This is why I urge others to seek Him in this regard. I know that what He has done for me He will do for all those who call upon Him in truth.

Knowing the Word of God can do much to keep us free from fear. His Word is filled with wonderful promises. To you, He says:

The angel of the Lord encamps around those who fear Him, and He delivers them. Psalm 34:7

If you can learn to fear God, to reverence Him, to hold Him in awesome respect, you will have no reason to fear others, and this promise can be yours. His angels will camp around you, protecting you from every enemy. Trials will still come and bad things may still happen, but you have nothing to struggle about — if you are leaning on the Lord. He will give you victory over every enemy. Ask Him, then trust Him, to work for you.

Chapter Ten

Doing the Works of God — Through Christ

I can do everything through him who gives me strength.   Philippians 4:13

Because God is with us, and we have entered into a convenant relationship with Him, He has given us the privilege of acting in His name. We are to do His works, by sharing in His strength.

Theoretically, we know that this is true, for God doesn't lie. But realistically, we also know that there are times when we are forced to confess to God, "I have no energy. I'm scared. I don't even know where to start."

It is in those moments that we need to look beyond our limitations and tap into His unlimited strength and ability, recalling the promise: *"I can do everything through Him who gives me strength."*

You may find yourself in a job situation that is way over your head. If so, you may be feeling completely overwhelmed with it all. Most of us have experienced it at one time or another. Cry out to God, confessing your inability and seeking His ability, and you will be surprised how quickly He comes to your rescue.

Our Lord is so gracious in these situations. He knows what we can handle, and He delights in giving us His strength. He delights in pouring out to us His grace. He delights in providing everything necessary to help us through our most difficult situations.

It is best not to wait until a crisis before we seek God. The ideal is to seek Him daily and to know going into every situation that we are being guided by His light and reinforced by His strength. Whatever we face, He is with us and will give us His ability to do what we need to do.

When we think of this promise, first given to the Philippians, we usually place the emphasis on our ability to do *"everything,"* or as the King James Version renders it, *"all things."* In the original Greek, however, the emphasis is very different. A more literal translation of the verse might be:

> *I can do everything that God demands of me through the power of Christ who is resident within me.*

136

Doing the Works of God — Through Christ

The Living Bible says it this way:

I can do everything God asks me to with the help of Christ who gives me the strength and power.

Philippians 4:13, TLB

It's not that we can just do anything we want to do. We can do everything that God is asking of us. When He asks a particular thing of us, He obligates Himself to enable us to do that thing.

The word *strengthens* here is a very important one. It literally means, "the power of God that is resident within us." It is this power of God that enables us to do what He requires of us.

In view of the fact that God places His ability within us and enables us to do *"everything,"* Paul urged the first-century Christians to *"offer [their] bodies as living sacrifices ... to God":*

Therefore, I urge you, brothers, in view of God's mercy, to offer your bodies as living sacrifices, holy and pleasant to God — this is your spiritual act of worship. Do not conform any longer to the pattern of this world, but be transformed by the renewing of your mind. Then you will be able to test and approve what God's will is—His good, pleasing and perfect will.   Romans 12:1-2

When we fully submit ourselves to God, He not

only makes His will known and understood to us, but He enables us to *"test and approve"* it. Don't be afraid. Say to Him: "Lord, I submit my body to You, as a living sacrifice. I want to be transformed so that my mind is renewed to think Your thoughts and so that my hands can do Your works." You have nothing to lose and everything to gain.

Paul continued:

> *For by the grace given me I say to every one of you: Do not think of yourself more highly than you ought, but rather think of yourself with sober judgment, in accordance with the measure of faith God has given you. Just as each of us has one body with many members, and these members do not all have the same function, so in Christ we who are many form one body, and each member belongs to all the others. We have different gifts, according to the grace given us.* Romans 12:3-6

Although we can do the works of God, through His enablement, we have nothing of which to boast. All the glory goes to Him; nevertheless we can be endued by God with special gifts and abilities that will abound to the building of His Kingdom, to the development of His Body on the earth. God is gracious to give us all that we need to accomplish His purposes for us and through us.

Usually, what keeps us from working the works

of God is not some external force, but our own humanity. The psalmist saw us as people on a pilgrimage through a valley filled with trials:

> *Blessed are those whose strength is in You,*
> *who have set their hearts on pilgrimage.*
> *As they pass through the valley of Baca,*
> *they make it a place of springs;*
> *the autumn rains also cover it with pools.*
> *They go from strength to strength,*
> *till each appears before God in Zion.*
> *For the Lord God is a sun and shield:*
> *the Lord bestows favor and honor;*
> *no good thing does He withhold*
> *from those whose walk is blameless.*
> *O Lord Almighty,*
> *blessed is the man who trusts in You.*
>
> Psalm 84:5-7, 11-12

The King James Version renders verses 11 and 12 in this way:

> *For the Lord God is a sun and shield; the Lord will give grace and glory: no good thing will He withhold from them that walk uprightly. O Lord of hosts, blessed is the man that trusteth in Thee.*

Our God has all that we need, and He imparts His goodness to us as it is required. If you need grace, He will bless you with grace. If you need His glory, that is His manifest presence, He will come to you. He will do whatever is necessary so that He is reflected in us and through us. We can work the works of God — in spite of ourselves — if we trust in Him.

"The Valley of Baca," spoken of in verse 6, was "a place of misery and tears," signifying a place of sorrow, crises, and pain. But the psalmist declared that we are only to *"pass through"* that valley. We are not intended to stay there. None of God's children should have to live in a place of weeping or pain or sorrow. God's healing can lift us out of misery, as we declare to Him: "My hope is in You, Lord. My trust is in You. I'm not able to release this pain to You, so please take it. I can't do anything about it, but You can. Change this place that I am in from a place of sorrow to a place of springs, a place of blessing. Take my tears, and replace them with blessing and gladness so that I can show to the world that You are alive. Give to Your people the ability we need to overcome in every situation and to do everything You require of us."

That type of surrender is the central message of this psalm. Those whose strength is in God, who have set their hearts on the fact that they are in a pilgrimage, are on their way to a better place.

We have no reason to put down roots in the Valley of Baca, no reason to stay there the rest of our lives. Don't be like those who have taken up permanent residence, wrapping themselves in self-pity, in continual mourning and in tears.

The Lord is saying to us, "Come, My people, pass on through. Make your life a pilgrimage, and don't stay too long in the Valley of Baca. Trust Me to put My ability in you so that this place will be turned into a place of gladness, a place of blessing, a place of springs."

If you are determined to pass on through the valley and not become mired in its suffering, you too can go from strength to strength, as you draw on the resources of God.

This process of gradual maturing through God's ability is also seen in the New Testament:

But we all, with unveiled face beholding as in a mirror the glory of the Lord, are being transformed into the same image from glory to glory, just as from the Lord, the Spirit.

2 Corinthians 3:18, NAS

If you have made that determination to press on in God, He is changing you *"from glory to glory."* As we behold Him, we can say, "O God, it's You in whom I trust. I cannot do this thing by myself. I can't let go of the pain, the resentment, the anger, the hatred. I cannot let go of the grief without Your help. But, Lord, I have chosen to put my eyes upon You."

As we look to our Lord, we are changed, more closely conformed to His image. When Paul wrote that we are changed *"from glory to glory,"* he meant that we begin to reflect the brightness of our God, while we are still here on the earth, with all its difficulties.

This does not depend on our being perfect, and sometimes that is our problem. We want to be perfect, and we are disappointed when we aren't. We think, "I've really messed up. I've fallen. I've done things that I ought not to do, and I can't seem to do any better." God speaks to us, in our concern. He says:

> *The steps of a good man are ordered by the Lord: and He delighteth in his way. Though he fall, he shall not be utterly cast down: for the Lord upholdeth him with His hand.*
>
> Psalm 37:23-24, KJV

Sometimes we feel that this scripture could not apply to us, because it refers to *"the steps of a good man,"* and we may not be feeling very "good" at the moment. But we are not "good" by our own goodness; we are "good" because of His goodness, which is resident in our lives.

When we receive Jesus as our Savior, He takes up residence in us. While our righteousness was nonexistent, God now looks at us through the righteousness of Christ, and we qualify for His blessings.

Could this verse hold true even when we seem to fail over and over again? Let the Scriptures answer:

> *For a just man falleth seven times, and riseth up again: but the wicked shall fall into mischief.*
>
> Proverbs 24:16, KJV

Does such a thing as *"a just man"* even exist? Yes! A just man is someone who is trying to live a good life through God's grace. Even though such a one may fall seven times, he will surely rise again. Micah speaks to this matter, as well:

> *Do not gloat over me, my enemy! Though I have fallen, I will rise. Though I sit in darkness, the Lord will be my light.*
>
> Micah 7:8

Micah was determined. He has resolved to press on and follow God — no matter what. And we must be just as determined. Even if you have fallen, you cannot give up. God can lift you up, and He can give you His strength. Reach out to Him today. Let your determination be: "I may have failed, I may have fallen, but I will not stay down long. I am determined to go on with God!"

Staying down would be the easy way out. Wallowing in self-pity is a convenient escape, but it is not a solution. Don't worry about being knocked down again. Get up. Stand to your feet. You are the chosen of God. Press on, and trust Him to help you. Humble yourself before the Lord, and He will lift you up again, as He has promised:

> *Humble yourselves before the Lord, and He will*
> *lift you up.* James 4:10

Perhaps your valley is one of deep despair. The prophet Habakkuk spoke to this:

> *Though the fig tree does not bud*
> *and there are no grapes on the vines,*
> *though the olive crop fails*
> *and the fields produce no food,*
> *though there are no sheep in the pen*
> *and no cattle in the stalls,*
> *yet I will rejoice in the Lord,*
> *I will be joyful in God my Savior.*
> Habakkuk 3:17-18

We don't need self-pity. We need a determination to overcome and to rejoice and be joyful in our God. Rejoicing is not just a feeling that we may or may not have. We can exercise praise as a matter of the will. God has given to each of us a mind and a will. Use that gift! Determine that you will not stay in the Valley of Baca, that place of weeping and tears and mourning. Determine to rejoice in God. Determine to excel — through His ability, not yours.

Many of us tend to get bogged down, trying to do too many things at once. Our contemporary culture tells us we can do it all, have it all, and be it all. We just need to learn to manage our time, our finances, and our talents more efficiently. If we fall for that logic, we may allow ourselves to work in too many directions at once. Jesus warned us of the dangers of this lifestyle:

> *Be careful, or your hearts will be weighed down with dissipation, drunkenness and the anxieties of life.*   Luke 21:34

One definition of this word *dissipation* is "the aimless scattering of one's energies." Think about that. If we are doing things God has not directed us to do, we can get off track and dissipate our energies aimlessly. His promise of strength and ability is for things He directs us to get involved with — not for our own agenda. Learn to keep focused on what God wants you to do.

Along with focus, we need fellowship. When our enemy comes to discourage us and cause us to lose that focus, we need others in the Body of Christ who will stand by us and encourage us to stay true to God's calling. We all need true friends who will pray for us and minister to us and help us to do all that

God is calling us to. The call to such fellowship is strong in the Scriptures:

> *Encourage one another daily, as long as it is called Today, so that none of you may be hardened by sin's deceitfulness.*　　　　　Hebrews 3:13

We need to encourage one another *"as long at it is called Today,"* which is every day. None of us can walk this walk alone, and that's why God has placed us together in the Body.

The writer of the Hebrews continued:

> *We have come to share in Christ if we hold firmly till the end the confidence we had at first.*
> 　　　　　　　　　　　Hebrews 3:14

"We have come to share in Christ." We are partakers of Christ; we are covenant partners with Almighty God through Jesus Christ ... *"if we hold firmly till the end the confidence we had at first."* We're going to make it — in spite of ourselves.

CHAPTER ELEVEN

BORN WITH A PURPOSE — THAT'S US

And we know that in all things God works for the good of those who love Him, who have been called according to His purpose. Romans 8:28

Because we are joined to God through covenant, we are a people of purpose, and we must discover God's purposes for our lives.

God calls us *"according to His purpose"* — both His purpose for His Kingdom and His purpose for our lives individually. We each have a purpose in life, a purpose that may be far above our imaginations. Our Father has a vision for each of us, a specific work for us to do, and we can fulfill that vision — with His help.

The purpose for your life was established before the foundation of the worlds. God has something specific for you to do, something that, no doubt, has not yet been totally fulfilled. So each of us must keep reaching out to find and fulfill our purpose.

To work toward God's purpose for your life, you must do it today. You cannot always live in tomorrow. It is one thing to make fine plans, but if we don't carry out those plans, we accomplish nothing. Today is the day for progress.

The plans you make must also be inspired of God. Your plans may be good ones, but unless they coincide with God's purpose for your life, they will bear little fruit. It is not wrong to ask God to help us to accomplish certain things that we want to do personally, but if the things we are doing are not in keeping with His plan, what can we expect to be accomplished over the long run? Trust God that He knows best for your life and seek His plans, rather than developing your own.

What Paul continued to teach the Romans is relevant in your life, as well:

> *For those God foreknew He also predestined to be conformed to the likeness of His Son, that He might be the firstborn among many brothers. And those He predestined, He also called; those He called, He also justified; those He justified, He also glorified.* Romans 8:29-30

You are predestined to greatness, and the predestined purpose of God for your life can be fulfilled only as you are *"called," "justified,"* and *"glorified."* The greatness of your potential can be realized only as you are *"conformed to the likeness of His Son."* Much of what God is doing in our lives daily has that purpose, to conform us to the image of Jesus. We need to stop struggling against the forces God uses to do this work in us. Relax and let Him mold you as He wishes.

We actually have two choices in life: we can be conformed to this world, the easy choice that most people make, or we can reject the pressure to constantly conform and choose to be like Jesus. It is a choice of self-will or death to self, which is what God still requires of us. This is not an easy choice for many, but it holds untold rewards for each of us who is willing to make it.

"Why is God asking us to do so much?" some might ask. He's not asking us to do so much. He did it all for us. He gave His life for us. He shed His blood for us. He gave everything for us. All He is asking is that we recognize those facts and let Him do for us what we cannot do for ourselves. He is prepared to take us on to greatness.

Paul's words were written to *"those who love Him,"* and that makes all the difference. If you love Jesus and make Him Lord of your life, by letting Him make decisions for you, it is not a burdensome thing. It is delightful. Jesus said:

Why Do We Struggle So?

If you love Me, you will obey what I command.
John 14:15

This is the test of our love for God: a willingness to obey Him in all things because we trust His judgment implicitly.

Jesus went on to add a wonderful promise:

And I will ask the Father, and he will give you another Counselor to be with you forever — the Spirit of truth.
John 14:16

The purpose of the *"other Counselor,"* the Holy Spirit, in our lives, is to help us conform to the image of Christ, to make us willing to trust His judgment and to enable us to obey Him without question or without feeling that what He is asking is an imposition on us. If we make the wrong decision in this regard, it is a serious matter:

He who does not love me will not obey my teaching.
John 14:24

Another translation of the phrase *will not obey* is "will ignore." It is possible to simply ignore the Word of God. If you take this path, you must know what the Bible frankly and clearly declares. It is a sign that you don't really love God.

If we really love Him, how can we mistrust His

eternal purposes for our lives? If we really love Him, how can we question what He desires of us? If we really love Him, how can we *not* obey Him?

Some say that they love God and then go on their merry way, doing exactly what they want to do from day to day, and ignoring God's will and purpose for their lives. We can only say that these people are either deceived or deceivers — or both.

Our loving heavenly Father has an established order, an eternal purpose and plan, and that established order requires specific timing:

> *There is a time for everything,*
> *and a season for every activity under heaven.*
>
> Ecclesiastes 3:1

> *He has made everything beautiful in its time. He has also set eternity in the hearts of men; yet they cannot fathom what God has done from beginning to end.*
>
> Ecclesiastes 3:11

Long before the worlds were formed, God had established His purposes and the timing of everything that would happen to bring about those purposes.

He has *"set eternity in [our] hearts,"* and we know that there is more to life than the nitty gritty of our daily existence. That isn't to say that we are required to live in misery now, in order to gain some future reward. He wants His children to be happy *now*. He wants us to enjoy all the benefits of His Kingdom right here on the earth.

The call of eternity in our hearts causes us to sense the timing of God and to move with that timing. It has been my privilege, in recent years, to preach the Gospel in Russia and in the Ukraine, with amazing results. People who had never before heard the Good News eagerly received the Word and were saved by the hundreds and by the thousands. I was amazed myself and could only conclude that it was the timing of God.

God had gone before us and prepared the hearts of the people. They had a God-sized void in their lives and were crying out for something real to cling to. God knew all that and sent us — just at the right time.

Auditoriums that should have held no more than a thousand people were packed with at least half as many more and sometimes twice as many more, and the people were eager to hear what we had to say.

What we preached was very simple. We did not waste time with eloquence. We told them that God loved them, that the relationship between God and man had been broken by sin, but that Jesus had come to reestablish that relationship through His sacrifice. "Jesus loves you," we told them, and they responded.

How privileged we were to be there, to participate in their salvation experience, and to see God's purpose for their lives and for ours, fulfilled! Nothing could have been more rewarding.

Most of us know instinctively that there is more to life than the things we see with our physical eyes. What we sometimes don't realize is that all we experience here on earth is just preparation for eternity.

We also fail, at times, to comprehend the seasons of our lives. At any given time, God is doing something very special in us. If we are faithful to walk with Him in that season, that particular time of preparation, He will take us forward to the next level.

Just as we go through weather cycles in the natural — spring, summer, fall, winter, and again, spring, summer, fall, winter — we have certain seasons of life that may be very different and, thus, confusing. Live one season at a time, and be faithful in that season — whatever it may happen to be.

If you are one of those who feel that they have no purpose in life, no reason to press on, you need to know that there is still something great for you to do, regardless of your age, regardless of your circumstances. God hasn't given up on you. He hasn't placed you on a shelf. He is still working on you and wants to work through you.

At one point in my life, I prayed that God would help me to love the unlovable. He answered that prayer by placing a neighbor in my life, a very un-lovable person, and someone who lived near us for the next thirteen years. Little by little, I was able to look past the unpleasant aspects of this man's appearance and his personality, to see his heart, a heart as big as the ocean. I came to love that man very much and, when he died, I grieved for him, and I missed him.

I later realized that if God had not placed that neighbor in my life, and if I had not asked the Lord to teach me to love him, a part of me would have gone unrefined and would have remained very much unlike the image of the loving Christ.

I haven't always recognized God's hand at work in my life. At times, in fact, I have stepped back and looked at the situations of my life and said, "There is no way that God could be in control of that." But I was wrong. He has it all under control and is reigning over the lives of those who love Him. In the end, we usually are able to see how a particular situation worked for our good, and, if not, we will understand in eternity that everything God permits in our lives is with a view to perfecting us in Him.

Some people turn to Christ and find themselves still yoked in marriage to an unbeliever. Although it may be due to some wrong choices on your part, God allowed that to happen. He knew that you would be brokenhearted, and He fully intends to do something about that. He sees your sleeplessness and your tears, and His heart is grieved. But, believe me, He has a purpose for it all. Trust Him and you will see something wonderful come forth from your present miserable situation.

Every heartache and every tear have an eternal purpose. God will turn your tears into pearls for His glory, for just as He has redeemed us, He will redeem the "situations" of our lives.

Some of us grieve over mistakes we have made. We grieve over lost time, lost opportunities, and lost possibilities. But God will even turn all of that to His glory. He is a God of restoration and knows how to take the time we have lost to sin, to error, and to aimless wandering and somehow use it for His eternal purposes, so that there is no loss in God.

My twelve years of wandering, of studying New Age doctrines, and of trying to find my own way certainly seemed like a lot of wasted time when I looked back on it. But God has taken even that and turned it to His glory. I have a deep hatred for that which is false and a deep love for that which is of God. The experience has made me a much stronger Christian and able to help many others.

Since I have known Christ, my life has not been perfect, but I know that every experience has led me closer to the goal of being like Christ. We are like wet mud poured into a mold. In time, we take on the shape of the mold. As we dry or mature, that shape becomes stronger and stronger, until eventually it is difficult to change. Isaiah wrote:

> *This is the plan determined for the whole world;*
> *this is the hand stretched out over all nations.*
> *For the Lord Almighty has purposed,*
> *and who can thwart Him?*
> *His hand is stretched out,*
> *and who can turn it back?*   Isaiah 14:26-27

There are times when we feel that Satan has somehow thwarted the purposes of God for our life, but that is simply not so. According to the promises of Scripture, it is impossible for Satan to stop God's purposes. He might slow things down by placing obstacles in our way, but ultimately, God is in charge, and there is nothing Satan can do to stop us from fulfilling our destiny — if we remain true to God. Nothing can happen to us unless the Lord permits it to happen, in which case, we know that something good will result.

We can't always explain why bad things happen to good people. We can't explain why some people seem to suffer more than others. There is a lot that we can't explain. But that doesn't change the fact that God is good and that His children are destined for greatness — despite the circumstances they face along the way, or perhaps, better said, *because* of the circumstances they face along the way.

Born With A Purpose — That's Us

In God, we shall be victorious. There may arise some giants in our lives — depression, fear, hatred, resentment, divorce, bankruptcy, sickness, accidents, etc. — and they may try to hinder. But while the giants are at work, God is also at work — whether we see Him working or not — and the outcome is assured. We are predestined to greatness in God.

I once read a story about a man watching his young son at play. He stood back, giving the boy space, allowing him to feel his independence. The little boy ran back and forth, playing with two or three of his friends. Suddenly, the child fell down and skinned his knee. What happened?

The father, who had never taken his eyes off the little one, rushed to his aid, picked him up, and dusted him off, held him tightly as he cleaned and bandaged the hurt and comforted his son. But he didn't hold him this way forever. After the child was comforted, cleaned up and attended to, he put him down again, and the child ran off to play, as before.

Would we ever say that this man was interfering in his son's life? Hardly. He intervened only when he was needed. Otherwise, he let the child play. He was, however, ever vigilant and came immediately to the child's rescue in his time of need. This, to me, is a picture of our heavenly Father. This is the way He has manifested His love in my life.

He will never leave us, never turn His back on us. And He preserves our lives from danger so that we can fulfill His eternal purposes:

I am God, and there is no other.
I am God, and there is none like Me.
I make known the end from the beginning,
from ancient times, what is still to come.
I say: My purpose will stand,
and I will do all that I please.
From the east I summon a bird of prey;
from a far-off land, a man to fulfill My purpose.
What I have said, that will I bring about;
what I have planned, that will I do.

Isaiah 46:9-11

You are made for a purpose. You are cut from a divine mold, and God will not permit anything to happen in your life that will rob you of your destiny. To you, it may seem, at times, as though everything is lost. You may wonder if your life has ended and if there is any reason to go on. It is in those moments that you need to turn to God's Word and refresh your sense of His promises:

He who began a good work in you will carry it on
to completion until the day of Christ Jesus.

Philippians 1:6

God is not through with you yet, and if you continue to trust Him, His eternal purposes will be fulfilled in your life.

CHAPTER TWELVE

FAITH
— THE GREAT HINDRANCE REMOVER

And, behold, there was a woman which had a spirit of infirmity eighteen years, and was bowed together, and could in no wise lift up herself. And when Jesus saw her, He called her to Him, and said unto her, Woman, thou art loosed from thine infirmity. And He laid His hands on her: and immediately she was made straight, and glorified God. Luke 13:11-13, KJV

Although, as children of God we possess such great promises, many members of the Body of Christ are just like this woman before her encounter with our Lord that day. Their heads are bowed to the ground, rather than lifted toward Heaven. They've grown discouraged. They've lost hope. They've given up.

What Jesus said to this woman is so significant: *"thou art loosed."* The work is finished. The snare of the enemy has been broken. We are free. We just need God to put His finger under our chins and lift our faces toward Heaven, so that we can see the truth of our deliverance. We just need to accept, by faith, the finished work of the cross.

On another occasion, two blind men were following Jesus, crying out, *"Son of David, have mercy on us!"* They followed Him into the house where He was staying, and a conversation ensued:

> *Jesus saith unto them, Believe ye that I am able to do this?*
> *They said unto Him, Yea, Lord.*
> *Then touched He their eyes, saying, According to your faith be it unto you.*
> *And their eyes were opened.*
>
> Matthew 9:28-30, KJV

"According to your faith be it unto you." It isn't enough merely to give mental assent to the fact that God is on our side and that He is willing to fight our battles. An intellectual comprehension of the blood covenant is insufficient, in itself. You may know, in theory, that you can walk in freedom from bondages such as fear, but it is not enough. Each individual must lay hold of all these blessings — through faith in God.

Faith — the Great Hindrance Remover

It is possible to believe that God is good and still not be sure that His goodness will be displayed in my own life. I must believe Him that what He has done for Abraham, He will do for me. I must know Him, not just as the God of Abraham, Isaac and Jacob, and the God of Paul and Barnabas and Timothy, but the God of Carol Richardson, as well. I must have faith in God for my own need.

Faith! All of us need more of it. The Scriptures declare:

So then faith cometh by hearing, and hearing by the word [rhema] of God.   Romans 10:17, KJV

Our faith comes as we hear the *rhema* [word] of God — the specific word that He speaks to us as individuals. The *logos* [word], the entire written Word of God, is settled and will never change. We can read it and appreciate its many values. It has historic value, prophetic value, and inspirational value. But unless God comes by His Holy Spirit and brings that *logos* to life for us, the Bible is much like any other important document.

When the Holy Spirit breathes upon a particular passage and makes it real to us personally, that scripture becomes a *rhema* word to our hearts. The *rhema* word, then, is simply the *logos* word upon which God Himself has breathed life for our particular situation. When that happens, lay hold of it; thank God for it; believe it; walk in it; and never let it go.

We need the *rhema* word of God to build our faith. We need to have the breathed-on Word of God made life within us so that our faith may grow. If Christ said to the blind men, *"According to your faith be it unto you,"* there is no reason to believe He doesn't say the same to us today:

_____, *according to your faith be it unto you.*

Put your own name in that space.

The only thing limiting you in God is your faith or the lack of it. You must personally know the promises of the Word of God, and you must make them your own.

The first important thing that must be said about understanding the Word of God is that it is impossible to do it without first understanding the One who wrote it. You must enter into an intimate relationship with God Himself and spend time with Him, if you ever hope to understand His promises to you.

Take time to get into your prayer closet and seek Him. You will find Him waiting there, and He will respond to you as you pray. As you draw near to Him, He will draw near to you. Knowing Him more intimately will help you to understand His Word so that you can believe for Him to finish what He has started in you.

Everything you face in your daily life is an opportunity for you to exercise your faith in God, and every time you do it, your faith increases.

I am convinced that we spend far too much time rehearsing our problems to one another and talking about the difficulty of our situations, and not nearly enough time pondering the Word of God and its promises. If we would speak God's promises over our situations, instead of dwelling on the problems and difficulties that lie in the pathway, we could see more clearly that what seems like a problem is really an opportunity for God to gain glory and for our personal faith to grow.

When some promise from the Word of God has been made alive to us, we can declare that promise over our lives and all that we have. He has destined us for blessing to all those with whom we come in contact.

As you read any part of the Bible, apply the promises made there to your own life. As long as you are fulfilling the conditions to the promise, God has not changed. As the Scriptures show us, He is *the same yesterday, today, and forever*" (Hebrews 13:8). The miracles and the promises of which we read in every part of the Bible are still valid for believers today. God's power has not diminished in the least!

God cannot do any more than He presently is doing. We are not waiting on Him to move, but He is waiting on us to believe and receive. This is our responsibility. We must learn the Word and believe for its practical application in our own lives. It is not enough to know that God has said something. I must know how to lay hold of that word for my personal situation. Every promise in the Book is mine — if God breathes life into it for me, and if I receive it by faith.

When I came back to the Lord in 1971, I didn't know any good Bible teachers, so I just read and read, and kept on reading, the Bible for myself. As I was faithful to do this, the Holy Spirit, who is the true Teacher, began to make the Scriptures clear to me. He remains faithful to teach as I remain faithful to study.

Because of my own experience, I am sure that the Spirit of God is faithful to teach all those who are willing to make the effort to learn. I can say without doubting that He will make the Word alive to you — if you will give Him the time He deserves. Do this, and God will begin to create in you a strong, bold, and confident faith that what He has done for others He will do for you.

The Bible is not a spiritual buffet laid out for us, from which we pick and choose what appeals to us. It is not given to us to arbitrarily believe or not believe, as we choose. This Holy Book is all good and to be applied to our lives.

God may quicken different sections of the Word to me from what He quickens to your spirit. He knows our needs. That decision is His alone.

As you read the Bible and come upon its great

promises, there are several helpful things you can do. First, read the promise in its context to make sure you understand all that God is saying. Parts of verses, taken out of context, can be used to prove just about anything.

Secondly, look for any conditions God has placed on the promise. Then see if you have fulfilled those conditions. If you have understood the promise in its correct context, and you have fulfilled any conditions attached to it, then cling to the promise, by faith, and trust God to fulfill it in your own life.

There exists what the Scriptures call *"the trial of our faith"*:

> *That the trial of your faith, being much more precious than of gold that perisheth, though it be tried with fire, might be found unto praise and honour and glory at the appearing of Jesus Christ.*
>
> 1 Peter 1:7, KJV

Don't despise or fear this trial. Everything of value must be tested and proven, and God has a right to test our faith. Just be assured, that as tests and trials come your way, your heavenly Father intends you no harm. He is only proving you and preparing you for promotion.

Keep your faith strong — whatever else happens. Don't concentrate on the problems. Hold fast to God. Meditate on His goodness. Know that He is on your side and that He will fight for you. He is bigger than any problem that may come your way. He is stronger than any snare that has been laid for you by your enemies. He is greater than any pit that has been dug for you to fall into.

God is great! Remind yourself of that fact from time to time. Our God is an awesome God. Hear His Word:

> *Lift up your heads, ...*
> *that the King of Glory may come in.*
>
> Psalm 24:7

He comes in to expectant hearts, to those who eagerly welcome Him.

God is not only the Author of our faith; He is also its Finisher. He is the One who has promised, the One with whom we have made a covenant, and because He is faithful and true, He will surely bring every promise to fulfillment.

He finishes what He has begun:

> *He who began a good work in you will carry it on*
> *to completion until the day of Christ Jesus.*
>
> Philippians 1:6

If God has begun a good work in you, rest assured that He will finish it. Lay hold of this great promise, and you will prosper.

Faith — the Great Hindrance Remover

Before God is finished with you, you will look like Jesus, act like Jesus, talk like Jesus, and even smell like Jesus. He wants the fullness of the character of Christ to be formed in you, and whatever it takes to accomplish that is exactly what God will do. He wants you as part of His spotless Bride, and whatever He has to do to bring you to that place, He will do it. Believe Him for it.

You may be one of those who have difficulty believing God because you have failed Him at some point. Always remember that the promises of God are not based on your goodness, but on His. Come back to God, and you are eligible for His goodness.

He has not forgotten you, even for a moment. He knew exactly how long it would take for you to mature and to be trained in righteousness when He called you, and He has never rescinded that call. He set out to make you like His Son, and He will not stop until His work in you is completed.

You may slow His work down for a while, and you might even be able to halt it—for the moment. When this happens, some well-meaning people may write you off as a loss. But as far as God is concerned, He is not only able to complete His good work in you ... He is committed to it. Nothing can change that fact.

So, take off all the restraints, and let God do His work in your heart. Let Him live His life in you and through you. If He can use me, I guarantee He will use you. God has used me to bless people all over the world and when God anoints me to teach His Word, even I am amazed. I know, in fact, that I can do *"everything"* through Christ — if my faith stays high. This is not self-confidence. It is God-confidence.

He is everything that we need Him to be. Why should we be fearful or cowardly? Our Master is all-powerful. That gives me courage to do His bidding. I may not be all that I can be now, but He is all that I need, and if I continue in Him, He will perfect me day-by-day:

> *The Lord will perfect that which concerneth me.*
> Psalm 138:8, KJV

Another way we can build our faith is to use the Scriptures in prayer. We might say: "God, Your Word says this to me. You have given me this promise, and I believe it. I trust in You and in Your Word. Therefore I trust that my enemy will be defeated. I will trust you, O God, knowing that my children will be delivered from the hand of the evil one, for Your Word says that *the seed of the righteous shall be delivered"* etc.

Lay hold of the Word of God in prayer. It has the potential of releasing great bursts of spiritual energy into your life and will give you faith to stand in even the most difficult situation. If we are faithful to spend time with God and in His Word, He will do the rest. David sang:

> *In the day when I cried Thou answeredst me, and strengthenedst me with strength in my soul.*
>
> Psalm 138:3, KJV

This reality of the Word bringing such vibrant life to our spirits is difficult for some to understand, but it should not be. After all, He was the Word made flesh, and He has indwelt the sacred Bible with His own presence. It is not the memorization of phrases that gives us power, but the fact that Christ, the hope of glory, is dwelling in us when we fill our hearts with His anointed Word and His Holy Spirit.

Let your faith rise so that you can lay hold of every promise and defeat every enemy — to the glory of God.

CHAPTER THIRTEEN

FULFILLING OUR PART OF THE BARGAIN

Love the Lord your God with all your heart and with all your soul and with all your mind and with all your strength. Mark 12:30

Being in covenant with the Lord means much more than getting all you can get from God. It also includes our commitment to Him. In covenant, we pledge all that we are and all that we have to the Lord of Hosts. And if we are truly walking in covenant, we will fulfill the command to love Him with *"all [our] heart[s] and with all [our] soul[s] and with all our mind[s] and with all [our] strength."*

As His representatives on the earth, He expects us to walk in holiness and repentance, to be good stewards of our time and resources, and to demonstrate our faith in Him daily. We are to seek Him in prayer, to worship Him from the heart, and to minister His love to others. And we are to do it all with confidence, never forgetting the promise of Isaiah:

The Lord longs to be gracious to you.

Isaiah 30:18

Because of God's great love, we can be all that He has called us to be. We can walk with our heads held high in confidence. We belong to the King of kings and Lord of lords. Someone very powerful is on our side. Someone very capable fights our battles.

Don't be afraid of that word *holiness*. It doesn't mean perfection, as some imagine. It means "set apart to God," nothing more. It means you have made a conscious decision to live for God — come what may.

We don't automatically become perfect when we receive Jesus Christ. Walking in the fullness of this covenant is a learning process. Although God is calling us to live a holy life, a life that reflects His glory, He is patient with us — as long as we're progressing, as long as we are going in the right direction. If we are dying to self daily, allowing Christ to live in us and through us, God is pleased. He is looking for a people that will say, "I want to do what You want me to do, Lord. I want what You want for my life." That is what it means to walk in holiness, yielding yourself to Him.

Fulfilling Our Part of the Bargain

Peter puts it this way:

> *His divine power has given us everything we need for life and godliness through our knowledge of Him who called us by His own glory and goodness.* 2 Peter 1:3

You will make mistakes, but God's forgiveness is infinite. The only time you will not be forgiven is when you don't ask to be forgiven. If you become so totally hard-hearted, so rejecting of God's Holy Spirit that you actually blaspheme Him, refusing the fact that you are a sinner and that you need Jesus Christ, then you are in trouble. The only *unforgivable sin* is not asking for His forgiveness.

You will be tempted, but when you are tempted, cry out to God for help. His ear is attuned to your cry. He affirms:

> *The eyes of the Lord are on the righteous and His ears are attentive to their cry.* Psalm 34:15

> *The Lord is far from the wicked but He hears the prayers of the righteous.* Proverbs 15:29

When you say, "God, help me!" He will answer, "I'm stronger than any temptation. Nothing can defeat you because I am with you." He delights in helping you in this way:

Why Do We Struggle So?

*The Lord your God is in your midst, a victorious
warrior.
He will exult over you with joy,
He will be quiet in His love,
He will rejoice over you with shouts of joy.*

Zephaniah 3:17

In the same way, we must delight in our experience with the Lord, never feeling that we are missing something important by giving Him our lives. The opposite is true. Those who fail to give their lives to Christ are missing His blessing in this life and will miss the life to come.

Our greatest responsibility here on earth is to believe in Jesus. This believing is not simply a mental affirmation or agreement with the facts concerning Jesus' earthly life and ministry. When you truly believe in someone, you place your whole trust in that person. God wants us to trust wholeheartedly in Jesus Christ and to maintain that trust until the end.

His part was in giving Himself for us. Now our part is to receive what He did for us. Why not do your part today? Say to Him:

Lord Jesus,

*I believe that You died for me and that my sins
were nailed to Calvary's tree. Since You have already paid for all my wrongdoings, help me to receive Your forgiveness and Your salvation.*

Amen!

Fulfilling Our Part of the Bargain

If you have sincerely prayed this prayer, you have become a joint-heir with Christ. His salvation is yours! That word *salvation* means much more than forgiveness of sins. It means that God wants to redeem you in every way — spiritually, physically, emotionally, and financially. His salvation is of the spirit, of the soul and of the body.

Ask Him to guide you to a local church where you can be baptized in water and further instructed. You need to be joined to a family of brothers and sisters in Christ who can help you grow strong in the Lord.

As He has taken your sins, let Him also take your burdens, your illnesses, your family struggles, and your financial difficulties. Be free in every sense:

> ... *those who are led by the Spirit of God are sons of God. For you did not receive a spirit that makes you a slave again to fear, but you received the Spirit of sonship. And by Him we cry, "Abba, Father." The Spirit Himself testifies with our spirit that we are God's children. Now if we are children, then we are heirs — heirs of God and co-heirs with Christ, if indeed we share in His sufferings in order that we may also share in His glory.* Romans 8:14-17

If you have made the decision to become a child of God, by faith in Jesus Christ and have received

His indwelling Spirit, you now have the Lord of the Universe, the Creator of all things seen and unseen, the Mighty Lord of Hosts living within you. You can say like the Apostle Paul:

> *If God is for us, who can be against us?*
>
> Romans 8:31

He is willing to fight our every battle, supply our every need, comfort and protect us. Whatever you are going through, whatever situation you find yourself in, remember that you have a blood-covenant God who is ready to come to your aid. He is wiser, stronger, and more equipped for battle than we could ever be. He wants to defeat our foes and set us on a pathway to total victory in life.

So ... why do we struggle so? Let's allow Him to do what we cannot do for ourselves. And to God be the glory!

Amen and Amen!

— Notes —

— Notes —

— Notes —

— Notes —

— Notes —

To contact the author for revivals,
retreats or conferences, write:

Carol H. Richardson

CHR Ministries
P.O. Box 255
Bath, NC 27808